ELOGOS

Daily Devotions for Down-To-Earth Disciples
3

Deb Grant

ELOGOS

DAILY DEVOTIONS FOR DOWN-TO-EARTH DISCIPLES 3

BY DEB GRANT

Copyright © 2015 by Debra Grant
Printed in the United States of America

All rights reserved. No part of this book may be reproduced or transmitted in any form or by any means without written permission from the author.

Scripture quotations from *New Revised Standard Version of the Bible* @ 1989 by the National Council of Churches of Christ in the USA. All rights reserved: used by permission.

Cover design: Debra Grant
Front cover photo: Erika Abel
ISBN: 978-0-9824226-2-5

To my Goddaughter
Alexandra Abel

Acknowledgements

I got it in my head that I would publish a 3-Volume set of ELOGOS devotions. This is the third and final volume of that commitment. Those of you who know what it means to make a promise to yourself and actually keep that promise know the joy I have at this moment. ELOGOS has been a part of my writing life for over 20 years. ELOGOS was originally created for the college students at Texas A&M University.

I am deeply grateful to my friends who encouraged my writing. There are readers who I have never met who often drop me an email with an encouraging word, a suggestion, or insight. Boots Jewel has gently nudged me into finishing this volume. Cats Sonnenburg has also been a relentless nag, an encouraging friend and my most willing copy reader. Heath & Erica Abel are friends who inspire me to greater joy than I deserve.

I cherish all the subscribers to the ELOGOS devotions who daily attend to God's Word through the discipline of reading ELOGOS. They represent hundreds of vocations and relationships. They serve God, each in their own way. They allow me the privilege of walking with them in their lives of faith and my own faith is strengthened because of them.

I pray that my goddaughter, Alex, will continue to enjoy the God who loves, chases and splashes her life with grace and purpose now and always.

Deb Grant

Introduction

ELOGOS first took the form of emails to students at Texas A&M University in College Station where I served as a campus pastor. The word 'logos' in Greek means 'Word' and more specifically, God's Word. The 'E' first stood for email. For this book, 'E' stand for 'every day.' ELOGOS 3 is part of a 3-volume set of yearly devotions.

For a generation who is accustomed to the shortness of text messages, I have intentionally kept the messages brief, but I hope that they have a long lasting effect. Most of the scripture selections were chosen on the basis of the text suggested by the New Revised Common Lectionary. I wrote each meditation on a word or phrase that rose to the surface as I read them each morning. I consider myself a "pedestrian theologian" – one whose faith is a journey alive in God's Word and alive in the down-to-earth experiences of daily life.

I pray that these bits of scripture, my humble words and earnest prayers will be a blessing to you wherever you are on your journey of faith.

Deb Grant

JANUARY ◆ 1

Isaiah 43:1a-4
Do not fear for I have redeemed you; I have called you by name, you are mine. When you pass through the waters, I will be with you; and through the rivers, they shall not overwhelm you; when you walk through fire you shall not be burned, and the flame shall not consume you. For I am the Lord your God, the Holy One of Israel, your Savior. I give Egypt as your ransom, Ethiopia and Seba in exchange for you. Because you are precious in my sight, and honored, and I love you, I give people in return for you, nations in exchange for your life.

❖ ❖ ❖

The image of passing through the waters was a rich one for the people of Israel. The story of Moses and Pharaoh were passed from generation to generation. Moses was leading for the sake of God's people. Pharaoh was leading out of anger and self-serving control. God had Moses' back. God has our back for no other reason than that he loves us. To trust in Him means that we are free to lead and help others.

❖ ❖ ❖

Holy God, thank you for your vigilance in watching over us so that we may honor your love through our selfless service. Amen.

JANUARY ◆ 2

Psalm 29:3-5
The voice of the Lord is over the waters; the God of glory thunders, the Lord, over mighty waters. The voice of the Lord is powerful; the voice of the Lord is full of majesty. The voice of the Lord breaks the cedars; the Lord breaks the cedars of Lebanon.

❖   ❖   ❖

I was playing with a child's toy. It was a plastic container for catching bugs for the purpose of observing them. It was a high-tech version of an empty jelly jar. It had a magnifying glass built into the lid and a special base that housed a microphone and with earphones one could listen to a bug scrambling across the surface. The problem was that the microphone also picked up external noises including my own breathing and my voice. My voice sounded like I could break trees and send a herd of cattle stampeding. I felt very sorry for the bug if my voice really sounded like that to it. To tell you the truth, sometimes I wish God's voice would sound EXACTLY like that so that we would all pay attention. But God's voice takes something beyond the vibration of our eardrums to recognize. God's voice sounds like hope and strength. God's voice sounds like love.

❖   ❖   ❖

Holy God, speak to us so that we will truly listen. Amen.

JANUARY ◆ 3

Isaiah 62:1-4
For Zion's sake I will not keep silent, and for Jerusalem's sake I will not rest, until her vindication shines out like the dawn, and her salvation like a burning torch. The nations shall see your vindication, and all the kings your glory; and you shall be called by a new name that the mouth of the Lord will give. You shall be a crown of beauty in the hand of the Lord, and a royal diadem in the hand of your God. You shall no more be termed Forsaken, and your land shall no more be termed Desolate; but you shall be called My Delight

❖ ❖ ❖

A soon-to-be bride arrived at a pre-counseling session wearing her bridal tiara with her street clothes. She said she wanted to wear it for more than just one day. We may laugh at that but it speaks more truth about all of us. We would love royal treatment - to be treated like princesses and kings. Claiming royal status for ourselves, however, never achieves what our souls need. To be lifted up to nobility by one who deserves it more than we ever will is truly a wonder. We carry around the burden of labels of our lot in life, namely "forsaken" and "desolate." But God calls us "My Delight." God delights in us. The very idea that we can make God smile from the inside out is a kind of royalty that lasts more than a day.

❖ ❖ ❖

God of Glory, we delight in your name and rejoice that your love and grace is so available. Amen.

JANUARY ◆ 4

Psalm 36:5-10
Your steadfast love, O Lord, extends to the heavens, your faithfulness to the clouds. Your righteousness is like the mighty mountains, your judgments are like the great deep; you save humans and animals alike, O Lord. How precious is your steadfast love, O God! All people may take refuge in the shadow of your wings. They feast on the abundance of your house, and you give them drink from the river of your delights. For with you is the fountain of life; in your light we see light. O continue your steadfast love to those who know you, and your salvation to the upright of heart!

❖   ❖   ❖

There is a line from the hymn "Glories of Your Name Are Spoken" that I have always liked. The last stanza says, "Savior, since of Zion's city I through grace a member am, Let the world deride or pity, I will glory in your name. Fading are the worldlings' pleasures - all their boasted pomp and show; Solid joys and lasting treasures None but Zion's children know." There is a vastness to God's love and mercy that the psalmists often try to capture - in the images of skies and clouds, mountains and seas. We also have the prairies and farmlands that stretch out beneath and endless, changing ceiling of color and light. This is just the beginning of the glory of God. Even more amazing is that such a God cares for each of us with the same breathtaking wonder.

❖   ❖   ❖

Wow, Lord, Wow!

JANUARY ◆ 5

I Corinthians 12:4-7
Now there are varieties of gifts, but the same Spirit; and there are varieties of services, but the same Lord; and there are varieties of activities, but it is the same God who activates all of them in everyone. To each is given the manifestation of the Spirit for the common good.

❖   ❖   ❖

It was a running joke in my house when I was growing up. Whose Christmas present would Mom forget to put under the tree and in what month would she find it? It was predictable that one of the children would be handed a perfectly wrapped Christmas gift in the middle of June. They were forgotten clutter hidden underneath a bed or in the c closet until they were turned into joy by being discovered and given. The old saying says that "love isn't love until you give it away." The gifts that we are given by God are meant to be given and are for the edification of the community. We have a responsibility to discover and know our gifts and the world is waiting to receive them from us.

❖   ❖   ❖

Lord, make us mindful of the gifts that are wrapped inside of each of us for the sake of others. Amen.

JANUARY ◆ 6

1 Peter 1:19
So we have the prophetic message more fully confirmed. You will do well to be attentive to this as to a lamp shining in a dark place, until the day dawns and the morning star rises in your hearts.

❖   ❖   ❖

Epiphany means manifestation of the light. The light was revealed to the world through Jesus Christ. That Good News is communicated to people the same way it did when Jesus first came - one person at a time. Just like the candlelight at a Christmas Eve service is lit from candle to candle so we are call to attend to the light given to us and make it available through us for others. Think about the times in your life when the person of Jesus Christ became real for you. It may have been an "Ah-ha!" moment or simply a warm realization that God's grace and forgiveness is real. As we attend to the light of Christ, the morning star rises for us all.

❖   ❖   ❖

Shine, Jesus, shine that we may see the good we can do in sharing that light with others. Amen.

JANUARY ◆ 7

John 13:34
Just as I have loved you, you also should love one another.

❖   ❖   ❖

Our lives are complicated. Our solutions to problems are even more complicated. Even our life of faith, the activity of the institutions of the Church, the decisions and stands we take in these times are complicated. There is a sweet simplicity to Jesus' commandment that blows through the din of our noisy complications. Love one another. We can hear the beginnings of our own protests. We can feel the "But, Lord..." about to erupt from our faces. Love, yes, but Lord - it is just not that simple. What does it mean to love? What do I have to do? What does love require of me at work, in my family, in my relationships? We want love dissected for us so that we can examine its parts and determine if such parts could truly be used in a mechanism such as the human heart. Perhaps with some alterations and an owner's manual and some classes, we could manage it. Yet the commandment is simple and carries with it confidence that we can, in fact, love. Could it really be that simple?

❖   ❖   ❖

Lord, simply love us that we might do the same. Amen.

JANUARY ◆ 8

Nehemiah 8:10
Then he said to them, "Go your way, eat the fat and drink sweet wine and send portions of them to those for whom nothing is prepared, for this day is holy to our Lord; and do not be grieved, for the joy of the Lord is your strength."

❖ ❖ ❖

A friend recommended a book to me that her family enjoyed. It was a book about a dog. I didn't want to read it. I had a dog who had been my loyal companion for 14 years. She died and I had not been able to read a dog book or watch a dog movie without turning into a puddle. But it had been 10 years since my Tugger died. It occurred to me that to deny myself the joy of a good book for fear of the pain did not seem like the holy life God gave me to live. We have plenty to grieve and fear without looking too hard. We can try to be positive on our own, but we quickly run out of steam and become whirling vortices of bitterness. Strength for another day is rooted in the God who loves us relentlessly.

❖ ❖ ❖

God, make this day holy with your joy and strength. Amen.

JANUARY ◆ 9

Psalm 19:14
Let the words of my mouth and the meditation of my heart be acceptable to you, O Lord, my rock and my redeemer.

❖   ❖   ❖

We all have trust issues. We can't function through a day without having to trust someone or something. We all know what it feels like to be hurt, betrayed, disappointed or tacitly misunderstood. Trust relationships that have been damaged between individuals take work to repair if there is any hope. Ignoring the problem means we have given up hope that the relationship is worth redeeming. Worse yet is when we have lost trust in our own ability to hear God's voice and obey it when we do. With such an earthquake of shattered trust happening around and within us, God offers us himself as our rock to steady our disquieted souls and our redeemer to give us hope that righteousness can be born within our hearts and become words that can lead others to an unshakable Savior.

❖   ❖   ❖

It's already a good prayer, Lord....Let the words of my mouth and the mediation of my heart be acceptable to you, O Lord, my rock and my redeemer. Amen.

JANUARY ◆ 10

I Corinthians 12:20-23
As it is, there are many members, yet one body. The eye cannot say to the hand, "I have no need of you," nor again the head to the feet, "I have no need of you." On the contrary, the members of the body that seem to be weaker are indispensable, and those members of the body that we think less honorable we clothe with greater honor, and our less respectable members are treated with greater respect; whereas our more respectable members do not need this.

❖ ❖ ❖

No Christian community during the early Church caused more hair-ripping frustration for Paul than the group in Corinth. They were contentious, smug, posturing with self-importance and oh-so-sure they were right...about everything from theology to food. We may be thousands of years removed from Corinth, but familiar to a fault with their antics. The scriptures coax us all back to good behavior. We all need one another. All members are to be valued. Instead of dismissing those who have behaved dishonorably, we are encouraged not to play the game of tit-for-tat but stop the cycle. We stop it by showing honor to those least deserving of honor. Very, very difficult to do. Paul will go on in his letter to define love in proportions that stretch our imaginations but hopefully our hearts as well. Love bears all things, believes all things, hopes all things...even when it is very, very difficult to do.

❖ ❖ ❖

Lord, you bid us walk the high road with you. Give us the will and courage to follow. Amen.

JANUARY ◆ 11

Luke 4:17-21
And the scroll of the prophet Isaiah was given to him. He unrolled the scroll and found the place where it was written: "The Spirit of the Lord is upon me, because he has anointed me to bring good news to the poor. He has sent me to proclaim release to the captives and recovery of sight to the blind, to let the oppressed go free, to proclaim the year of the Lord's favor." And he rolled up the scroll, gave it back to the attendant, and sat down. The eyes of all in the synagogue were fixed on him. Then he began to say to them, "Today this scripture has been fulfilled in your hearing."

❖ ❖ ❖

It was one of those moments when you could safely say that Jesus had their attention. What he did with that attention was to remind them of Israel's past when they did not listen and when others showed more compassion and understanding of God's word than they did. Within 7 verses after the scene described in this Luke passage, the people who had listened to him so intently literally wanted to throw him off a cliff. Jesus moved on. He did not try to defend himself or save his job. He just moved on to another town to preach again the same word of conviction and freedom. It is a painful and wonderful moment when we realize that we are the captive and sightless. We are the mob keeping at a distance the one who offers us all freedom and sight.

❖ ❖ ❖

Lord God, today let us rediscover who you are to us. Amen.

JANUARY ◆ 12

I Corinthians 9:22-23
To the weak I became weak, so that I might win the weak. I have become all things to all people, that I might by all means save some. I do it all for the sake of the gospel, so that I may share in its blessings.

❖ ❖ ❖

There is much emphasis these days on individual freedom especially the right to speak. Paul's message of being willing to lose himself for the sake of communicating the message of the gospel may seem foreign. What would it take for us to believe in a cause so deeply that we would abandon our individuality, our nature, our freedom for the sake of the privilege to meet people where they are? To listen deeply without preparing our next words is a form of self-sacrifice that is the beginning of what it takes to proclaim the gospel. The proclamation doesn't begin with words but with the willingness to stand empty and meet that person where they are, not where we want them to be. The world could use more listeners.

❖ ❖ ❖

Holy God, help us to listen for the sake of your gospel. Amen.

JANUARY ◆ 13

Jeremiah 1:4-8
Now the word of the Lord came to me saying, "Before I formed you in the womb I knew you, and before you were born I consecrated you; I appointed you a prophet to the nations." Then I said, "Ah, Lord God! Truly I do not know how to speak, for I am only a boy." But the Lord said to me, "Do not say, 'I am only a boy'; for you shall go to all to whom I send you, and you shall speak whatever I command you, Do not be afraid of them, for I am with you to deliver you, says the Lord."

❖   ❖   ❖

Jeremiah is referred to as the "melancholy prophet." He had a miserable job to speak to a people who were misbehaving to tell them God wasn't happy and things were going to get worse for them before they would get better. Jeremiah spent most of his prophet career complaining about his task. God had to drag him kicking and screaming, whining and pouting to his people. Of the mouthpieces for the Lord, one would think God could have chosen better. But the ones who had the least agenda seemed to be the ones who took some care in getting the words of God to the people exactly how God meant them to be delivered. Along the way, the Lord never left Jeremiah. When we find ourselves whining and complaining, it is good to know that the Lord may not change the circumstances for all our whining but our whining can never drive him away.

❖   ❖   ❖

Lord God, it's not fair...it's not fair...it's not fair....but thanks for listening. Amen.

JANUARY ◆ 14

Psalm 71:1-4
In you, O Lord, I take refuge; let me never be put to shame. In your righteousness deliver me and rescue me; incline your ear to me and save me. Be to me a rock of refuge, a strong fortress, to save me, for you are my rock and my fortress. Rescue me, O my God, from the hand of the wicked, from the grasp of the unjust and cruel.

❖   ❖   ❖

Growing up in a 3-bedroom/1-bath house with 5 other people, I spent a lot of time trying to find places to hide. I hid under tables, beds, bushes, cardboard boxes, behind doors and in trees. Sometimes I needed to be alone, but there were plenty of times I needed to be found. We all need those places or those people who can be our hiding place, who will shelter us in our vulnerability and respect our space but not leave us alone. Sometimes we hide when we need to be found. Sometimes we don't know what we need but even in our confusion we are surrounded by a God who protects us while we rediscover him.

❖   ❖   ❖

Lord God, thank you for giving us the freedom to hide and the protection of your grace. Amen.

JANUARY ◆ 15

I Corinthians 13:4-7
Love is patient; love is kind; love is not envious or boastful or arrogant or rude. It does not insist on its own way; it is not irritable or resentful; it does not rejoice in wrongdoing, but rejoices in the truth. It bears all things, believes all things, hopes all things, endures all things.

❖ ❖ ❖

I read these words over and over again. They sound so good. It reads like poetry and sounds like a song. Part of me wants to be loved like that and another part of me wants to believe that I can love like that. I am reminded that I am and I can....not because of any great effort or wisdom or willpower but because I can't help it. There is something about standing in the presence of God that turns us into vehicles for his blessing and purposes whether we like it or not. God is the love that courses through our veins and turns love into things beyond our ability to create ourselves...patience, humility, long-suffering, strength.

❖ ❖ ❖

God of love, teach us who you are so that we might be the vehicles for your amazing grace. Amen.

JANUARY ◆ 16

John 4:29
Come and see a man who told me everything I have ever done!

❖   ❖   ❖

"What was one of your most embarrassing moments?" It is a good conversation starter because we all have stories. I wet my pants when I was a pre-school child as a guest on a local children's television program. That moment didn't bother me nearly as much as years later when my mother retold the story to my teenage friends. We move around in our lives knowing that we make mistakes, but we spend an enormous amount of energy covering up those mistakes. Motivated by fear or embarrassment, we hide acts that reveal our vulnerability or weakness. The idea of a God who knows everything there is to know about us is frightening. The woman at the well encounters Christ who tells her everything she has done. It started out for her as an embarrassing moment, but became an encounter with her Savior.

❖   ❖   ❖

Lord God, Help us not fear of what you know about us and rejoice that you forgive us. Amen.

JANUARY ◆ 17

Isaiah 6:5-8
And I said: "Woe is me! I am lost, for I am a man of unclean lips, and I live among a people of unclean lips; yet my eyes have seen the King, the Lord of hosts!" Then one of the seraphs flew to me, holding a live coal that had been taken from the altar with a pair of tongs. The seraph touched my mouth with it and said: "Now that this has touched your lips, your guilt has departed and your sin is blotted out." Then I heard the voice of the Lord saying, "Whom shall I send, and who will go for us?" And I said, "Here am I; send me!"

❖ ❖ ❖

A pastor friend of mine said to me, "When I find myself standing in a hole, the first thing I tell myself is to 'Stop digging.' We spend a lot of energy asking why we are in the hole we are in or blaming the ones who have shoved us in this hole. We are slow to see the shovel in our own hands. The beginning of holiness (pun intended) is to recognize our part in creating the hole and accepting the severe mercy of God's grace to purify us, to burn out the poisons, to make us wholly as God intended. The only possible response is to offer ourselves completely to the Lord's will and the Lord's way. That step is not without fear or difficulty but it certainly beats digging a hole as big as a grave.

❖ ❖ ❖

Precious Lord, forgive us, heal us and make us wholly yours. Amen.

JANUARY ◆ 18

Psalm 138:3,7-8
On the day I called, you answered me, you increased my strength of soul. Though I walk in the midst of trouble, you preserve me against the wrath of my enemies; you stretch out your hand, and your right hand delivers me. The Lord will fulfil his purpose for me; your steadfast love, O Lord, endures forever. Do not forsake the work of your hands.

❖ ❖ ❖

I have a friend who keeps reminding me that God isn't finished with me yet. In the midst of the grief of life changes, I have been amazed at God's ability to grow muscles in my soul that I didn't know I had. The challenge is not to wallow in the past or to ignore the pain of grief but to walk through it. Using these new muscles, we are coaxed to move one step at a time through the valley of shadows leaning in God's direction.

❖ ❖ ❖

O Lord, for slowing your pace to meet us when we falter and extending your gracious hand, we give you thanks. Amen.

JANUARY ◆ 19

I Corinthians 15:9-10
For I am the least of the apostles, unfit to be called an apostle, because I persecuted the church of God. But by the grace of God I am what I am, and his grace toward me has not been in vain.

❖ ❖ ❖

Apostle Paul knew alot about sin and grace. I have been blessed in my life to know a few people who live inside the state of grace in such a way that I have learned from them. They are all people of great strength, fierce love and clear sense of purpose. But they are all people who are powerfully aware of the sins they have committed and the grace they have received in Jesus Christ. They live daily fully aware of their capacity to sin, but equally aware of the enormity of the cross. I can think of no more tragic life than to recognize one's own desperate need for forgiveness and walk away from the cross believing it is too small.

❖ ❖ ❖

Almighty God, abundant in love and alive with grace, convict us of our sin and convince us that we are forgiven. Amen.

JANUARY ◆ 20

Psalm 25:14-18
The friendship of the Lord is for those who fear him, and he makes his covenant known to them. My eyes are ever toward the Lord, for he will pluck my feet out of the net. Turn to me and be gracious to me, for I am lonely and afflicted. Relieve the troubles of my heart, and bring me out of my distress. Consider my affliction and my trouble, and forgive all my sins.

❖   ❖   ❖

It is the sad reality that we regularly abuse and take for granted the relationships of family and friends. The phrase, "friendship of the Lord" caught my attention for it is the last thing in the world I deserve. I often forget my friends' birthdays. They rarely hear from me unless I need something from them. I assume they will be at my beckoned call and have to suppress impatience when they expect me to be readily accessible. Yet I would be a sorry human being without their grace and laughter. All the more, I need the friendship offered by the one who can give me a clinic in how to be a gracious friend.

❖   ❖   ❖

Dear Friend, I love you more than even I know. Amen.

JANUARY ◆ 21

Psalm 72:1-4
Give the king your justice, O God, and your righteousness to a king's son. May he judge your people with righteousness, and your poor with justice. May the mountains yield prosperity for the people, and the hills, in righteousness. May he defend the cause of the poor of the people, give deliverance to the needy, and crush the oppressor.

❖ ❖ ❖

The job description of the king sounded clean and simple. Those kings of Israel who held to that simple mission of faithfulness to God and God's people were the ones whose names are still remembered. The great commission of Jesus Christ is a simple one to understand - "Make disciples." When talking recently to a parent of a teenager, I pondered how difficult it is to be both a parent and a teen today. It is difficult enough trying to raise children in the midst of the confusing sexual landscape, frightening availability of dangerous substances and rampant materialism. Trying to make disciples out of them as well is overwhelming. Even still, the champions that persist - whether kings or parents, titans of industry or teachers of children - are the ones who understand who God is, who they are in relationship to that God and what they have been called to do. And they simply remember those pure facts, every single day.

❖ ❖ ❖

Holy God, give us the strength to shoulder your Word of grace and truth into the world. Amen.

JANUARY ◆ 22

Ephesians 3:11-12
This was in accordance with the eternal purpose that he has carried out in Christ Jesus our Lord, in whom we have access to God in boldness and confidence through faith in him.

❖   ❖   ❖

In the book "The Prince and the Pauper" by Mark Twain, two young men discover how they resemble one another and trade places so they can experience their different walks of life. At the end, the prince playing the pauper must return to the throne to be king. The man who befriended the prince without knowing who he was is taken before the king. The man pulls up a chair and sits down. The guards fly at the man who showed such disrespect since no one sits in the presence of the king without permission. The pauper now prince and now king had given the man permission always to sit. The man trusted that the true prince would remember his promise and keep his word. He did. Our God is an awesome God and to diminish his majesty in order somehow to make him appear more accessible to us dishonors this awesome God. Instead, the Lord of Heaven and Earth in all his majesty gives us permission to sit, to linger with him, to come before him with boldness.

❖   ❖   ❖

Great and wonderful God, we come before you with humility and boldness, understanding who we are as sinners and who you are as merciful. We linger in your presence with love and peace. Amen.

JANUARY ◆ 23

Isaiah 42:1-3
Here is my servant, whom I uphold, my chosen, in whom my soul delights; I have put my spirit upon him; he will bring forth justice to the nations. He will not cry or lift up his voice, or make it heard in the street; a bruised reed he will not break, and a dimly burning wick he will not quench; he will faithfully bring forth justice.

❖   ❖   ❖

Some of the best school teachers I have ever known have this innate ability to hush a classroom of children without ever raising their voice. I have not mastered that ability. I usually yell a lot. I stand in wonder at the ones who have that kind of strong yet peaceful presence. The words of the prophet are given to us so that we can grow in our understanding of the nature of God. God is soft steel. We are not to fear his justice or underestimate his strength.

❖   ❖   ❖

God of power and love, we leap into this day with the confidence that we are leaping into your arms. Amen.

JANUARY ◆ 24

Mark 1:2-3
See, I am sending my messenger ahead of you, who will prepare your way; the voice of one crying out in the wilderness: 'Prepare the way of the Lord, make his paths straight.'

❖   ❖   ❖

There is something that tugs at our humanity at the sound of a child left alone. Perhaps it is some imbedded memory from our own infancy of waking in the night and finding ourselves in a jungle of darkness and piercing it with the only weapon in our arsenal - a cry. Who among us has not known what it means to stand alone surrounded by a crowd of misunderstanding? Perhaps God knew what would call us to attention would not be a louder noise, or an earthquake or thunder but a single voice crying in the wilderness. Our Savior came surrounded by all the darkness and misunderstanding that we have ever known and pierced it with himself so that we would not be alone.

❖   ❖   ❖

Holy God, help us to find your voice in the din of our days. Amen.

JANUARY ◆ 25

Matthew 3:16-17
And when Jesus had been baptized, just as he came up from the water, suddenly the heavens were opened to him and he saw the Spirit of God descending like a dove and alighting on him. And a voice from heaven said, "This is my Son, the Beloved, with whom I am well pleased."

❖ ❖ ❖

Most adults on a daily basis don't stress over the question "Who am I?" For good or for ill, there are those around us who are more than willing to answer that question for us. "You are She Who Will Help Me Find My Jacket Right Now" or "You are He Who Pays the Bills" We blaze through our days defined by who we are to others. When we have the luxury of reflective time, only then are we haunted by who we are to ourselves. Does anyone truly know us as people beyond what we can do for them? Before Christ's ministry began, he was defined by his heavenly Father as family, beloved and pleasing. Such is the gift of our baptism. Before we did anything to deserve it or prove ourselves unworthy of it, God answered the question of who we are. We are family, beloved and pleasing.

❖ ❖ ❖

Holy God, thank you for the scope of your incredible grace. Amen.

JANUARY ◆ 26

Isaiah 62:3-4
You shall be a crown of beauty in the hand of the Lord, and a royal diadem in the hand of your God. You shall no more be termed Forsaken, and your land shall no more be termed Desolate; but you shall be called My Delight Is in Her

❖ ❖ ❖

Names are often chosen more by the sound of the name than what it means. The meaning of a name might be fun to research, but is rarely the decision-making issue. After the movie, Dances with Wolves, came out, I thought having Native American names that meant something would be fun and interesting. I have a dear friend who I teasingly call -"Cheez-Whiz for Brains." There were days when he readily embraced the name but most of the time he bears the name of a hard worker, a loving husband, a caring family man, and one of the finest Christian gentleman I have ever known. When we are labeled lost, hopeless, good-for-nothing, we begin to live inside the name. Some labels we bring upon ourselves and others are leveled unfairly at us. God invites us to embrace our new name, our new identity - as his beloved sons and daughters.

❖ ❖ ❖

Holy God, give us a name that we can truly live with. Amen.

JANUARY ♦ 27

Isaiah 49:3-4
And he said to me, "You are my servant, Israel, in whom I will be glorified." But I said, "I have labored in vain, I have spent my strength for nothing and vanity; yet surely my cause is with the Lord, and my reward with my God."

❖   ❖   ❖

The prophet of the Lord felt the same things we face at home and at work - a sense that there is often a futility in what we do. The dishes, the laundry, the yard work is endless. It is difficult to see progress in our jobs. The prophet called by God for God's purpose still doesn't feel any glory in his labors. He pulls himself out of the funk by remembering that the cause and the reward are all wrapped up in God. Faith sometimes means gutting it up and getting on with the task trusting that the one who gives us the strength to gut it up will indeed make all things right.

❖   ❖   ❖

Holy God, grant us the strength to do your will and believe your promises. Amen.

JANUARY ◆ 28

Isaiah 43:4-5b
Because you are precious in my sight, and honored, and I love you, I give people in return for you, nations in exchange for your life. Do not fear, for I am with you.

❖ ❖ ❖

The Borg in the Star Trek series was an alien life form that was the most dangerous enemy throughout the series because it represented what we most deeply fear - being absorbed into a single collective and losing all that makes us unique and individual. From the time we were young, we struggle with what it means to be a valued member of the family or school group or work or the community. We question our importance. We wonder what or who would be affected if we never existed or fell through the cracks of a collective humanity. I thank God for the opportunity to speak the truth out loud - to say to one who is uncertain of their value that if they were the only person on earth - God would still send his Son to suffer and die to save them. It is an idea that never gets old. God isn't trying to create a Borg and erase our personality. God is trying to have a family and that requires a lot of relentless, unconditional love.

❖ ❖ ❖

Holy God, surround us with the certainty of your love so that we might not be crippled by our own self-esteem. Amen.

JANUARY ◆ 29

I Corinthians 1:4-7
I give thanks to my God always for you because of the grace of God that has been given you in Christ Jesus, for in every way you have been enriched in him, in speech and knowledge of every kind- just as the testimony of Christ has been strengthened among you- so that you are not lacking in any spiritual gift as you wait for the revealing of our Lord Jesus Christ.

❖ ❖ ❖

Paul wrote this letter most likely by dictating it to a scribe who scratched out the words with ink on scrolls of primitive paper or animal skins. The scroll was then carried many weeks by foot or horse cart to its destination. Communication has certainly changed. In a few clicks of a computer key I can send the whole Bible bouncing off satellites in space to the other side of the planet in seconds. No matter the tools of our communication, we still need to grow in our knowledge and our ability to articulate what it means to live a life of faith in Jesus Christ. Christ reveals himself through us for others. Sometimes that happens through our deeds but often, we still need to open our mouths and speak of what we know.

❖ ❖ ❖

Holy God, help us to be bold to speak your name and claim our faith in you. Amen.

JANUARY ◆ 30

John 1:35-39
The next day John again was standing with two of his disciples, and as he watched Jesus walk by, he exclaimed, "Look, here is the Lamb of God!" The two disciples heard him say this, and they followed Jesus. When Jesus turned and saw them following, he said to them, "What are you looking for?" They said to him, "Rabbi" (which translated means Teacher), "where are you staying?" He said to them, "Come and see."

❖   ❖   ❖

Every once in a while, the Bible gives us a reason to laugh. John tells two disciples, "There's the Lamb of God!" They take off and follow him but clearly at a distance until Jesus turns to ask them what they want. Probably uncertain themselves, they blurt out - "Where are you staying?" Imagine standing before the Messiah and getting so tongue-tied that all that comes out is a limp conversation starter. The first stumbling steps of discipleship are ones which are laced with faith, anticipation and lack of knowledge. As we spend more time and grow in the knowledge of the one we are following, faith is made strong. The disciples weren't titans of the faith at the get go. They grew that way. So do we.

❖   ❖   ❖

Holy God, give us the faith to follow and the will to learn. Amen.

JANUARY ◆ 31

Luke 7:9
When Jesus heard this he was amazed at him..."not even in Israel have I found such faith."

❖   ❖   ❖

I get amazed easily. I am amazed by gravity. I am amazed at the color of pansies. I am amazed by the smile of teenagers who have had the braces on their teeth removed. I don't expect to see Jesus easily amazed. Jesus is, after all, God's Son and has some degree of insider information. That information might not stand in the way of his awe and reverence of God's ways and God's word but amazement would be a stretch. Yet, even still, Jesus is said to be amazed by the faith of a person who believes that Jesus doesn't have to be physically present to make healing happen. This person believed that it could happen at Christ's command. Jesus is amazed by this man's faith. Those who cannot see the future and yet boldly believe and move toward that future are amazing.

❖   ❖   ❖

God of Grace, continue to amaze us with your power and strengthen our faith. Amen.

FEBRUARY ◆ 1

Isaiah 9:3-4
You have multiplied the nation, you have increased its joy; they rejoice before you as with joy at the harvest, as people exult when dividing plunder. For the yoke of their burden, and the bar across their shoulders, the rod of their oppressor, you have broken as on the day of Midian.

❖ ❖ ❖

What gives you joy? I never seem to have an answer for that on the tip of my tongue. I hesitate. I have to wrap my head around the word joy and define it. Sometimes the definition changes depending on the day and the setting. Taking a shower, listening to people sing, the sound of the unique ringtone of a friend, a cup of good coffee, a parent that teaches their children to write "Thank you" notes, a day without hearing any whiny voice especially my own. The list could go on but the answer would always depend on who wants to know and whether at that moment I am at peace inside my own skin enough to let joy happen. We have plenty of yokes and burdens that anesthetize our ability to know joy. Perhaps we can know some joy in the knowledge that God is working on those burdens.

❖ ❖ ❖

Holy God, for your relentless mercy in lifting our burdens, we give you thanks. Amen.

FEBRUARY ◆ 2

Psalm 27:4
One thing I asked of the Lord, that will I seek after: to live in the house of the Lord all the days of my life, to behold the beauty of the Lord, and to inquire in his temple.

❖   ❖   ❖

One thing. When it comes to our prayers, it rarely ever is "one thing." It may be lumped into a general plea for peace or patience or strength, but usually it is a whole list of things. The idea of living in God's house conjures up the image of putting our toes up in a recliner which is a luxury lots of people don't have. The psalmist is talking less about rest and more about the one thing that would make a difference in everything. The one thing is that his whole life could be powerfully lived in the constant awareness of God's nearness. The house of the Lord is a place without walls or a roof. It is, however, surrounded with the heartbeat, the strong arms and the breath of God.

❖   ❖   ❖

Holy God, make us aware of your attentive care in our lives. Amen.

FEBRUARY ◆ 3

I Corinthians 1:17-18
For Christ did not send me to baptize but to proclaim the gospel, and not with eloquent wisdom, so that the cross of Christ might not be emptied of its power. For the message about the cross is foolishness to those who are perishing, but to us who are being saved it is the power of God.

❖ ❖ ❖

The early Church was fighting over petty things like "who baptized whom." In a couple millennia since then, the Church hasn't gotten any less petty. God has patiently and firmly taken the church by the hand and, sometimes by the ear, in the form of prophets, teachers, and preachers who have lifted the Church beyond its squabbles to confront its mission in the world. God does not make our mission light so that we can attain it. He gives us an overwhelming task and the strength and wisdom to serve it. Wasting the energy God has given us on matters of little import is one of the great tragedies of the Christian community.

❖ ❖ ❖

Holy God, help us to serve you with courage and a focused mind. Amen.

FEBRUARY ◆ 4

Matthew 4:20-22
Immediately they left their nets and followed him. As he went from there, he saw two other brothers, James son of Zebedee and his brother John, in the boat with their father Zebedee, mending their nets, and he called them. Immediately they left the boat and their father, and followed him.

❖   ❖   ❖

Immediately....the word leaps off ancient text onto a printed page or computer screen or an e-book reader and grabs our attention. Either the sons of Zebedee were ready for change or there was something about this Jesus that made everything they were doing in that moment pale in comparison to him. Maybe it was both. The fact of the matter is that they followed. Being a follower of Jesus Christ means leaving too. We have to make room for the journey and that means letting go of a certain control that all of us wish we had in our lives. May we immediately recognize Christ when we see and hear him and trust him with our lives.

❖   ❖   ❖

Holy God, help us to ease off the strangle-hold we have on our days to be free to grab your hand. Amen.

FEBRUARY ◆ 5

Luke 5:31
Jesus answered, "Those who are well have no need of a physician, but those who are sick."

❖ ❖ ❖

Denial is one of the strongest muscles of a stubborn mind. We see the symptoms of a head cold but we deny that it is coming. We see the symptoms of troubled relationships but we rarely make a change to address the problem. We see the symptoms of a culture out of control but seldom take a stand for justice. Those of us who deny that we are the part of the problem create havoc for those around us. To move through our lives without the will for true repentance and the vocabulary of confession is to lose the relationships most dear to us. Our denial of our need and our sin is the ultimate burner of bridges. To deny that we need forgiveness means that we feel the breeze of Jesus passing by us to be with those who long for mercy. There is a hole in our lives the size of the cross and to deny the hole exists is death-dealing. Each day we are given the freedom to deny our emptiness or embrace the fulfillment of God's truth. Martin Luther's last words were "We are beggars. It is true." To such is the Kingdom given.

❖ ❖ ❖

Lord God, help us not to deny our need for the forgiveness and mercy. Amen.

FEBRUARY ◆ 6

Exodus 24:12-14
The Lord said to Moses, "Come up to me on the mountain, and wait there; and I will give you the tablets of stone, with the law and the commandment, which I have written for their instruction." So Moses set out with his assistant Joshua, and Moses went up into the mountain of God. To the elders he had said, "Wait here for us, until we come to you again; for Aaron and Hur are with you; whoever has a dispute may go to them."

❖ ❖ ❖

Come and wait and wait until we come. That's a whole lot of waiting going on. Don't the Lord and Moses know that we are busy people? Have the commandments ready when we get there or better yet, email them to me or send me a text message! What's with all this going up and down the mountain and making everyone wait. Maybe the waiting part was important. The next time we are forced to wait maybe we will discover what God had in mind and that perhaps we are not always the one doing the waiting.

❖ ❖ ❖

Holy God, may your wisdom and grace visit us in our impatience. Amen.

FEBRUARY ◆ 7

Psalm 2:3-6
The kings of the earth set themselves, and the rulers take counsel together, against the Lord and his anointed, saying, "Let us burst their bonds asunder, and cast their cords from us." He who sits in the heavens laugh s; the Lord has them in derision. Then he will speak to them in his wrath, and terrify them in his fury, saying, "I have set my king on Zion, my holy hill."

❖ ❖ ❖

There are moments when I trip over my own personal clutter of doubt. Perhaps we are all fooling ourselves about this God. It doesn't take much to start to unclutter it. A little bit of scripture, that story spoken from grandparent to grandchild or passed by messenger on ancient parchment from village to village. Those words invade my mess. Over and over again, it speaks of a God bigger than the silly plans of men and women. Again, it speaks of a God so big that everything humanity has done to squash, change, defeat or deny God's love has failed. We all want to be conquerors of our own realm. We need to learn to be satisfied with servanthood to the one who will always win miraculously enough because he loves us.

❖ ❖ ❖

Holy God, invade our day with your powerful presence and enormous love. Amen.

FEBRUARY ◆ 8

Genesis 1:1-5
In the beginning when God created the heavens and the earth, the earth was a formless void and darkness covered the face of the deep, while a wind from God swept over the face of the waters. Then God said, "Let there be light"; and there was light. And God saw that the light was good; and God separated the light from the darkness. God called the light Day, and the darkness he called Night. And there was evening and there was morning, the first day.

❖ ❖ ❖

Unlike the magician who redirects audience attention to accomplish a trick, God - not the creation - is the center of the Genesis event. God created. God swept. God said. God saw. God separated. God called. We spin our wheels about the science of it all. Science plays an important part. It seeks to answer "How?" That shouldn't direct our attention away from the voices of those who seek to help us answer the question, "Who?" The God who keeps the scientists busy at their discoveries is also busy. God lingers, a breath away from our own breath, ready to speak, to act, to listen and to love.

❖ ❖ ❖

Almighty God, creator of the universe, may we be a little less overwhelmed by the universe of our own making and more in awe of your gracious presence. Amen.

FEBRUARY ◆ 9

Matthew 17:5-7
While he was still speaking, suddenly a bright cloud overshadowed them, and from the cloud a voice said, "This is my Son, the Beloved; with him I am well pleased; listen to him!" When the disciples heard this, they fell to the ground and were overcome by fear. But Jesus came and touched them, saying, "Get up and do not be afraid."

❖ ❖ ❖

Bright lights, voices from clouds - that would have scared the willies out of anyone. Much has been written to conjecture about what they saw and why Matthew wrote what he wrote. What we do know is that the disciples were so shaken they lost their footing. It happens to all of us for a variety of reasons. We lose our footing and we are afraid. Jesus spends much of his ministry telling people not to be afraid. He is concerned about our fear because it stands in the way of a vibrant faith. We have alot to fear from our God who is as big as God is...but we have even more to know, love and celebrate.

❖ ❖ ❖

Almighty God, you are awesome. Grant us the boldness to linger in your presence without fear. Amen.

FEBRUARY ◆ 10

Luke 5:8-11
But when Simon Peter saw it, he fell down at Jesus' knees, saying, "Go away from me, Lord, for I am a sinful man!" For he and all who were with him were amazed at the catch of fish that they had taken; and so also were James and John, sons of Zebedee, who were partners with Simon. Then Jesus said to Simon, "Do not be afraid; from now on you will be catching people." When they had brought their boats to shore, they left everything and followed him.

❖ ❖ ❖

I was reading a book the other day that posed an interesting challenge: make a list of everything that you know is true. The truths for which the author was reaching were not simple truths like the sky looks blue or the size of our shoes. She was asking what we believe is true about our lives. Peter thought he knew the truth about fishing. Jesus told him where the fish were biting. Peter may have been obedient more to prove him wrong than out of faithfulness. Peter stood face to face with a man who not only knew the truth but who was the truest thing Peter had ever seen and it made him look like a fraud in comparison. Instead of leaving Peter groveling in the truth of his own inadequacy, Jesus invited him to follow him. We will never be our own great truth but recognizing the truth when we see it and following is not at all a bad way to live.

❖ ❖ ❖

Lord, help us to let go of our own pride and arrogance and follow you. Amen.

FEBRUARY ◆ 11

Leviticus 19:2
You shall be holy, for I the LORD your God am holy.

❖   ❖   ❖

So what do you want to be when you grow up? At various time in my childhood, I wanted to be a cowgirl, an archeologist, a professional Girl Scout, a Nobel prize winning author, a Navy officer, a tugboat captain and a hobo. I never aspired to be holy. Being holy sounds impossible. Being holy sounds boring but that is only because we equate sinning with fun and being good with being dull. Truth be told, we wouldn't know if being good all the time is boring because we've never done it! Holiness, however, is not a state of perpetual do-gooder-ness. Holiness is being set apart, one of a kind, designated as God's own. It is not something we can achieve like merit badges, but that which is given to us by God's speaking and making it so. God said we are holy. We are set apart for God. We manage to take some of the shine off of that holiness in a hurry but it remains a part of our official designation. We are members of a holy family and set apart. Growing up in that holiness is actually the fun part.

❖   ❖   ❖

Lord, make us live and breathe what it means to be your holy people in the world. Amen.

FEBRUARY ◆ 12

Jeremiah 17:8-9
Blessed are those who trust in the Lord, whose trust is the Lord. They shall be like a tree planted by water, sending out its roots by the stream. It shall not fear when heat comes, and its leaves shall stay green; in the year of drought it is not anxious, and it does not cease to bear fruit.

❖   ❖   ❖

It was an odd essay assignment that I had been given in high school. The task was to write my thoughts on the question "What is the opposite of a tree?" At first I thought only in substance and dimension.....something short and inorganic but that thought felt too ordinary. I decided that I myself was the opposite of a tree. I was rootless and wandering. I was uncertain of how anything could course through me and out my branches and produce fruit. I worried that I was not built to be marvelous only ordinary. The process convinced me that perhaps I needed to be more like a tree....trusting and patient and that I could not help but produce that which I was built to produce. Trust and patience seems so ordinary that we look for something more miraculous. Trust and patience inside a human being is miraculous.

❖   ❖   ❖

Lord, create in us the ability to wait with patience and trust your word. Amen.

FEBRUARY ◆ 13

Psalm 1:1-2
Happy are those who do not follow the advice of the wicked, or take the path that sinners tread, or sit in the seat of scoffers; but their delight is in the law of the Lord, and on his law they meditate day and night.

❖ ❖ ❖

I teach a peer ministry course which educates how to care for people effectively. There is one lesson that is always difficult. In order to minister well to peers who are struggling with a problem, telling them what they should do is not a good way to help. Giving advice takes away their freedom to choose for themselves. It also sends a message that they are unable to make a good decision. Better than advice-giving, helping a friend to explore their options and understand what is important to them, honors them as a person and respects their freedom. That's work. Blurting out advice is much easier. It makes us feel smart and powerful to know what the right thing is. If only people would listen to us, all would be right with the world. To consider the word of God is to discover that God's word rarely tells us what to do in every situation in which we find ourselves. The Bible doesn't tell us what to do in every situation. It tells us to follow Jesus. By doing so we have the freedom to discover who we truly are. When we value a right relationship with God, we can be confident in the outcome.

❖ ❖ ❖

Oh Master, let us walk with you in lowly paths of service true. Amen.

FEBRUARY ◆ 14

I Corinthians 15:17-20
If Christ has not been raised, your faith is futile and you are still in your sins. Then those also who have died in Christ have perished. If for this life only we have hoped in Christ, we are of all people most to be pitied. But in fact Christ has been raised from the dead, the first fruits of those who have died.

❖ ❖ ❖

During pre-marital counseling, I often ask couples to make a list of 10 specific things they like about the other person and 5 things that they don't like, but acknowledge they are willing to live with. The exercise is usually rewarding for both and an honest recognition. The things that drive them crazy about one another now will not change after marriage, but they are still committed to the whole person. There were those during the first century who would have preferred to order the "buffet" of Christian beliefs. Some in Corinth believed in everything about Christ but did not see the importance in the resurrection. There are those today who operate in the same mode. "I believe this but I don't like that..." But belief in Christ is not like a buffet line, it is more like a marriage. There may be some things about Christ that are more difficult to believe than others but our relationship with him means commitment to the whole person...not just a bundle of ideas.

❖ ❖ ❖

Holy God, we believe - help us in our unbelief. Amen.

FEBRUARY ◆ 15

Luke 6:18-19
They had come to hear him and to be healed of their diseases; and those who were troubled with unclean spirits were cured. And all in the crowd were trying to touch him, for power came out from him and healed all of them.

❖ ❖ ❖

One of the ways we can help other people who are struggling is to help them see and explore their options. The downward spiral of hopelessness and depression is often triggered by a sense that a person has no options. Those who contemplate suicide do so because they believe there are no other viable options. Modern medical practitioners are merchants of hope because they lay out an array of therapeutic or pharmaceutical or surgical choices. There were fewer possibilities in Jesus' time for those suffering with health problems. The hope of Christ's healing hand glistened. Today, too often, seeking Christ is more of a last resort. No matter if we choose him first or last, Christ still chooses us.

❖ ❖ ❖

Bless, O Lord, thy children in need of your word and healing and hope. Amen.

FEBRUARY ◆ 16

Psalm 25:14-18
The friendship of the Lord is for those who fear him, and he makes his covenant known to them. My eyes are ever toward the Lord, for he will pluck my feet out of the net. Turn to me and be gracious to me, for I am lonely and afflicted. Relieve the troubles of my heart, and bring me out of my distress. Consider my affliction and my trouble, and forgive all my sins.

❖ ❖ ❖

It is the sad reality that we regularly abuse and take for granted the relationships of family and friends. The phrase, "friendship of the Lord" caught my attention for it is the last thing in the world I deserve. I often forget my friends' birthdays. They rarely hear from me unless I need something from them. I assume they will be at my beckoned call and have to suppress impatience when they expect me to be readily accessible. Yet I would be a sorry human being without their grace and laughter. All the more, I need the friendship offered by the One who can give me a clinic in how to be a gracious friend.

❖ ❖ ❖

Dear Friend, I love you more than even I know. Amen.

FEBRUARY ◆ 17

Exodus 34:32-35
Afterward all the Israelites came near, and he gave them in commandment all that the Lord had spoken with him on Mount Sinai. When Moses had finished speaking with them, he put a veil on his face; but whenever Moses went in before the Lord to speak with him, he would take the veil off, until he came out; and when he came out, and told the Israelites what he had been commanded, the Israelites would see the face of Moses, that the skin of his face was shining; and Moses would put the veil on his face again, until he went in to speak with him.

❖   ❖   ❖

When Moses had been in the presence of the Lord, his face was shining so much so that it scared people. He put a veil over his face with other people and removed it in the presence of the Lord. Some scholars speculate that he did this because he knew that the shine on his face would fade and Moses didn't want the people to see the shining glory of the Lord on Moses' face fade. Moses removed the veil in the presence of the Lord because the glory of the Lord was something to behold. In our own relationship with God, we experience both the sensation of fear and the compelling attraction to be nearer to him. In the space in between our fear and his presence, we draw close to those whose countenance glows with the spirit of the Lord. We are blessed with a Moses or two in our lives who reflect God's glory on us.

❖   ❖   ❖

Lord God, send us those who reflect your spirit and may others see your face on us. Amen.

FEBRUARY ◆ 18

Jeremiah 31: 34
For I will forgive their iniquity, and remember their sin no more.

❖   ❖   ❖

One of the most important characteristics of God is that God chooses to forget. The fact that God can choose to forget in and of itself is an indication of God's divine power. Willfully forgetting a wrong done to us is simply beyond our power and even our comprehension. We are likely to say we forgive but cannot forget. Often we are not giving much more than lip-service to forgiveness. Forgiveness is always costly. Whether we need it ourselves or we need to offer it to someone else, the price of forgiveness is always the same - the life of God's Son. When we ask for forgiveness we are asking to wrap up our sin in the body of Christ. When we forgive, we wrap up the pain of the wrong done to us in the body of Christ. Though the memory of the wrong still may linger in our heads, the power of it has disappeared in the cross. Forgiving and forgetting is not as complicated as we seem to make it. We just need to trust God with the forgetting part and concentrate on the true meaning of forgiveness.

❖   ❖   ❖

Merciful Lord, forgive us as we have been forgiven. Amen.

FEBRUARY ◆ 19

Psalm 46:10
Be still, and know that I am God!

❖   ❖   ❖

Martin Luther was a German man who became a monk and for the first years of his life in the monastery he was consumed with his own depravity. The knowledge of his own sin was so deep that it sent him into the depths of depression and self-loathing. He began to be convinced that that nothing - including God - could be greater than his sinfulness. A wise mentor sent the young monk to study God's Word and to focus on the nature and character of God. He discovered that when he was willing to stop acting as his own judge and jury and let God be God in his life, there was hope for him. One of the continuing mistakes we make in our journey of faith is to imagine a God who is too small to overcome our sin. It happens when we forget that we are in relationship with God. In any relationship, it is always important to keep learning about each other. God makes himself known to us. When we are told to be still and know God, it is not meant as a chastisement, but a way to get our attention so that we can know the freedom and the grace that God gives us in Christ.

❖   ❖   ❖

Lord God, make us ever mindful that your cross is big enough to redeem the world. Amen.

FEBRUARY ◆ 20

Nehemiah 8:3
He read from it facing the square before the Water Gate from early morning until midday, in the presence of the men and the women and those who could understand; and the ears of all the people were attentive to the book of the law.

❖   ❖   ❖

The reading of the scriptures was so noteworthy that the prophets recorded the time and place. They spent hours listening to the Word. The words swirled around them and through them and sunk deep in to their consciousness, into the hidden crevices of their shadow lands. They marinated in God's word. It is difficult to imagine people today listening to someone reading out loud for hours. Even still, we must creatively seek ways in which we can allow the Word of God to soak into us so that it can become a part of who we are. Bibles are now digitalized and available in formats that make God's word as accessible as a cell phone or a tablet. The scriptures are read every Sunday in worship. May we choose to linger in it.

❖   ❖   ❖

Holy God, surround us with the life-giving power of your word. Amen.

FEBRUARY ◆ 21

Luke 9:33-36
Just as they were leaving him, Peter said to Jesus, "Master, it is good for us to be here; let us make three dwellings, one for you, one for Moses, and one for Elijah" -not knowing what he said. While he was saying this, a cloud came and overshadowed them; and they were terrified as they entered the cloud. Then from the cloud came a voice that said, "This is my Son, my Chosen; listen to him!" When the voice had spoken, Jesus was found alone.

❖ ❖ ❖

In the history of the people of God, Israel had a rich plethora of patriarchs, matriarchs, kings, poets and prophets. They were a host of witnesses. They were part of the storied history of God's people. The time had come, however, for one to stand out in the crowd. We lead complicated and busy lives. The din of global issues, tabloid queens, and terrorist regimes launch themselves in our direction. Priorities clamor for nothing less than the number one position for our energy and resources and time. Everything and everyone seems to have a value and looms with urgency and importance. With firm but gently awesome power, God shoves it all into the background and leaves Jesus standing front and center and alone. We look around and behind him for where everything and everyone else is. Again we are told, "This is my Son....listen to him." When we are looking and listening to him alone, we discover all that we have been looking for - and all that we are - inside a heart in which we ourselves....fit.

❖ ❖ ❖

Holy God, help us in the din of our days to see you alone as our salvation. Amen.

FEBRUARY ◆ 22

Deuteronomy 26:1-2
When you have come into the land that the Lord your God is giving you as an inheritance to possess, and you possess it, and settle in it, you shall take some of the first of all the fruit of the ground, which you harvest from the land that the Lord your God is giving you, and you shall put it in a basket and go to the place that the Lord your God will choose as a dwelling for his name.

❖   ❖   ❖

Giving God a cut off the top as a way to say thanks to God for all that he has done for us is part of the ancient tradition. It was habit that was instilled in the people of Israel from an early age. Considering what God has done for us, he could have asked for more. He could have asked for it all. But God only asked for 10 percent. During the season of Lent, we consider something we could give up or a task or project we could take on in order to walk with some integrity inside the suffering of Christ for us. Given that we are always Easter people moving toward the source of our grace and hope for eternal life, we could all do with a little less of ourselves.

❖   ❖   ❖

Holy God, remind us of all that you have given us today. Amen.

FEBRUARY ◆ 23

Psalm 91:1-4
You who live in the shelter of the Most High, who abide in the shadow of the Almighty, will say to the Lord, "My refuge and my fortress; my God, in whom I trust." For he will deliver you from the snare of the fowler and from the deadly pestilence; he will cover you with his pinions, and under his wings you will find refuge; his faithfulness is a shield and buckler.

❖   ❖   ❖

As a child, I loved watching "Mutual of Omaha's Wild Kingdom" and learning about the birds who would provide refuge under their wings for their young. I was even more in awe of the mother partridge who would pretend to have a broken wing and limp away from her nest in order to lead a predator away from it. No matter our age or our station in life, we do not grow out of the need for a refuge and a protector. Refuge for us takes the form of a chair in which we rest and pray, or time on the phone with a family member or friend, or space inside our cars where we can be alone with our thoughts. A protector is harder for us to invent or conjure up. Jesus is our protector and is able to surround us wherever we find our refuge.

❖   ❖   ❖

Holy God, surround us with your powerful arms that we might rest in thee. Amen.

FEBRUARY ◆ 24

Romans 10:14-15
But how are they to call on one in whom they have not believed? And how are they to believe in one of whom they have never heard? And how are they to hear without someone to proclaim him? And how are they to proclaim him unless they are sent? As it is written, "How beautiful are the feet of those who bring good news!"

❖ ❖ ❖

An exercise I have done with youth involves assigning each of them functions of parts of the body such as senses, arms and legs. They are not allowed to do anything but their assigned function and as a group they are given a simple task. Working together is a necessity. Suddenly a simple act of eating a cracker and taking a drink become monumentally complicated when several people have to move as one. Life is complicated. Relationships are complicated. Health is complicated. We regret and second-guess many things. Through all the complexities of this life, there is the simple act of bringing good news to a life that desperately needs good news. Good news is that Jesus Christ, the Son of God has died for us and is risen and offers us forgiveness of sin, freedom to love, and eternal life. Using our feet to walk through our complicated lives to deliver that news is a beautiful way to live.

❖ ❖ ❖

Holy God, we give you thanks for all the beautiful feet which have delivered the Good News to us. Amen.

FEBRUARY ◆ 25

Luke 4:5-8
Then the devil led him up and showed him in an instant all the kingdoms of the world. And the devil said to him, "To you I will give their glory and all this authority; for it has been given over to me, and I give it to anyone I please. If you, then, will worship me, it will all be yours." Jesus answered him, "It is written, 'Worship the Lord your God, and serve only him.'"

❖ ❖ ❖

The temptation of power is an insidious thing. No matter how diminutive our kingdom we seek to be able to control our immediate surroundings - particularly the people around us. We love ordering our animals to sit or stay and feel a small burst of power like an illegal substance shot into our veins. Left unchecked, the desire to have power over other people is only a heartbeat behind. We want all of the control but none of the work involved in understanding or being understood. We simply aren't innately kind when left to our own devices....we will lean in the devil's direction. The Word of God provides both the protection and the light for the perilous journey through our own self-serving tendencies.

❖ ❖ ❖

Protect us, O Lord, and guide our feet to the way of peace. Amen.

FEBRUARY ◆ 26

2 Samuel 7:11-12
From the time that I appointed judges over my people Israel; and I will give you rest from all your enemies. Moreover the Lord declares to you that the Lord will make you a house. When your days are fulfilled and you lie down with your ancestors, I will raise up your offspring after you, who shall come forth from your body, and I will establish his kingdom.

❖ ❖ ❖

I presided at the funeral of a family matriarch. She had ten children, countless grandchildren and great grandchildren. The family gathered. They grieved. They laughed. They were all different. They had this eternal thread which was woven forever within them all. When pulled, that thread could easily unravel the fabric as it could draw it closer together. The picture God gives us of the kingdom is of a family drawn together to be God's people. The kingdom of God is established in the connective tissue of our common roots in the one who gave us life and forgiveness and grace.

❖ ❖ ❖

Holy God, you knit us together in your family. Draw us from our separate lives into a fabric strong and everlasting. Amen.

FEBRUARY ◆ 27

Genesis 15:2-6
But Abram said, "O Lord God, what will you give me, for I continue childless, and the heir of my house is Eliezer of Damascus?" And Abram said, "You have given me no offspring, and so a slave born in my house is to be my heir." But the word of the Lord came to him, "This man shall not be your heir; no one but your very own issue shall be your heir." He brought him outside and said, "Look toward heaven and count the stars, if you are able to count them." Then he said to him, "So shall your descendants be." And he believed the Lord; and the Lord reckoned it to him as righteousness.

❖   ❖   ❖

This is one of my favorite stories in the scriptures because it is the beginning of the faith of Israel. God talks to one man and gives that one man a promise. That man doubts. God takes him outside to show him the stars. The man believes. I can see the scene play out in my head. I can imagine Abram's longing and his doubt. I can see him being led out of his tent...feeling the night air on his face as he looks up and sees the desert sky cloudy with stars. I can hear the thought sink into his soul- "Meet your family." I love that story. I love it because faith still happens one person at a time and God still keeps his promises. I love that faith can make a family and take away the loneliness of the night.

❖   ❖   ❖

Holy God, take us outside and show us our family numbered like stars that again we might believe we are not alone. Amen.

FEBRUARY ◆ 28

Psalm 27:11-14
Teach me your way, O Lord, and lead me on a level path because of my enemies. Do not give me up to the will of my adversaries, for false witnesses have risen against me, and they are breathing out violence. I believe that I shall see the goodness of the Lord in the land of the living. Wait for the Lord; be strong, and let your heart take courage; wait for the Lord!

❖ ❖ ❖

I led a group of mostly college students to the historical sites related to Martin Luther in Germany. The challenge of traveling there is always the language. Not knowing any German, I thought "Ausfahrt" was the biggest city in Germany because there were signs for it everywhere....until I found out that it means "Exit." Communication when we don't know the language complicates our living well. Communication when we DO know the language is still difficult. I have had words of mine twisted beyond recognition. I have been aware of the twisting process that operates inside my own sinful soul. The path to one another is never a clear one. When the lies are flying, and the path away from one another seems more perilous than the path toward each other, we steady ourselves on the strength of God's truth. We take courage and lean into the hard work of understanding each other. It is worth it.

❖ ❖ ❖

Holy God, teach us how to listen with understanding and speak with humility. Amen.

FEBRUARY ◆ 29

Philippians 3:20-4:1
But our citizenship is in heaven, and it is from there that we are expecting a Savior, the Lord Jesus Christ. He will transform the body of our humiliation that it may be conformed to the body of his glory, by the power that also enables him to make all things subject to himself. Therefore, my brothers and sisters, whom I love and long for, my joy and crown, stand firm in the Lord in this way, my beloved.

❖ ❖ ❖

I was saddened after reading a report that today's college-aged people are more narcissistic than ever. After decades of concerns about our human self-esteem, we have created a culture of self-absorption. We get caught in a cycle of self-importance to self-loathing and spending alot of energy swinging in between. That is the nature of this world. Jesus calls us to be citizens of heaven even as we tramp about in the cesspool of our own sinfulness. By being resident aliens, we are called to conform ourselves not to the chronically self-centered culture around us but conform to the Body of Christ. Our worth can be identified in the cross of Christ....the meaning of our lives can be identified in responding with thanksgiving to God by serving others.

❖ ❖ ❖

Holy God, keep us from turning so far inwardly that we snack on our own bones and lose sight of the feast of your Son. Amen.

MARCH ◆ 1

Genesis 3:8-10
They heard the sound of the Lord God walking in the garden at the time of the evening breeze, and the man and his wife hid themselves from the presence of the Lord God among the trees of the garden. But the Lord God called to the man, and said to him, "Where are you?" He said, "I heard the sound of you in the garden, and I was afraid, because I was naked; and I hid myself."

❖ ❖ ❖

In all of the scriptures there are few verses that are as tragic as these. The consequence of sin is a distant relationship from the one who created and loved us. Instead of reveling in the presence of God and running toward him, we run away. We hide. We cower. We declare that God is unnecessary. We claim God never existed. No matter how we try to be God, we are not very good at being God. We are still human and God is still God. We have no authority only the freedom to run and hide. The grace of it all is found in the God who seeks us out as we both hide and hunger for God's presence. The beginning of wisdom is the fear of the Lord.

❖ ❖ ❖

Holy God, call us from our hiding places with your relentless grace. Amen.

MARCH ◆ 2

Psalm 32:3-5
While I kept silence, my body wasted away through my groaning all day long. For day and night your hand was heavy upon me; my strength was dried up as by the heat of summer. Then I acknowledged my sin to you, and I did not hide my iniquity; I said, "I will confess my transgressions to the Lord," and you forgave the guilt of my sin.

❖ ❖ ❖

Ashes, ashes, we all fall down. Lent is a season of ashes that stops us in our tracks and reminds of what fragile packages of blood and tissue we are. Lent comes as surely as spring comes. It is not as confined to calendars as we might think. In that season of Lenten shadows, we feel the heavy weight of guilt that squeezes the breath out of us. The ashen season, however, does not call us to wear sad faces but to face ourselves and live. To confess our sins before a gracious God is the necessary daily movement from death to life so that we may share the Good News. We all fall down. The miracle of grace is that God does not leave us in the pile of our own making.

❖ ❖ ❖

Holy God, we remember that we are dust and to dust we shall return, but that isn't the end of the story. Amen.

MARCH ◆ 3

Romans 5:14-15
Yet death exercised dominion from Adam to Moses, even over those whose sins were not like the transgression of Adam, who is a type of the one who was to come. But the free gift is not like the trespass. For if the many died through the one man's trespass, much more surely have the grace of God and the free gift in the grace of the one man, Jesus Christ, abounded for the many.

❖   ❖   ❖

A virus moves with stealth and rides on such innocent gestures like a handshake or a computer file. Would if we could isolate the person who brings it into a community, but chances are, we would do more than isolate them for being a carrier. Jesus was killed for claiming to be God. He was also killed for being beautifully human. He exposed the ugly truth about our own humanity. Jesus died from our virus. So corrupt is our virus that if we were a computer, we would not be worth the sum of our parts. The power of God's love for the world that shone forth in the resurrection recreated us all. The infection still lingers but it has lost its ability to crash us. We are wise to the size of God's love and the ingenuity of God's salvation.

❖   ❖   ❖

Holy God, restore us to health and remove the power of sin from our lives. Amen.

MARCH ◆ 4

Luke 1:4
So that you may know the truth

❖   ❖   ❖

When we hear a truth told to us by a network news anchor or a Nobel prize winning scientist, we may not share that truth with another person. We hear a bit of unproven gossip from a trusted friend and we take the information to heart because we trust the vehicle. When we trust the messenger, we trust the message. Therein lays the power of God's truth when shared by a trusted friend. Luke was compelled to tell the story about Jesus. There is a hymn in which we sing "I love to tell the story because I know it's true." Those who saw the Risen Lord told the people what they knew and those people told people they knew. The truth about Jesus comes to us after hundreds of years in the same manner it came to those in the first century. The truth is shared from one person to another. It is as if the truth is so fragile and so wonderful that it cannot travel in its purest form through wireless signal or the internet. The truth about Jesus needs the vehicle of the human heart.

❖   ❖   ❖

Lord God, we cannot help but speak of what we have seen and heard. Amen.

MARCH ◆ 5

Romans 7:21-25
So I find it to be a law that when I want to do what is good, evil lies close at hand. For I delight in the law of God in my inmost self, but I see in my members another law at war with the law of my mind, making me captive to the law of sin that dwells in my members. Wretched man that I am! Who will rescue me from this body of death? Thanks be to God through Jesus Christ our Lord!

❖   ❖   ❖

Paul in his letter to the Romans and to us proclaims some of the most profound theology and faith in the scriptures. I like him for his honest description of our human battle with ourselves. We get in our own way. We trip over the cracks of our own sidewalk...and we keep tripping, very often in the same exact place. Paul is, by his own admission, a man of many cracks and much hope.

❖   ❖   ❖

Holy God, thanks for holding all our pieces together. Amen.

MARCH ◆ 6

Psalm 121:4-8
He who keeps Israel will neither slumber nor sleep. The Lord is your keeper; the Lord is your shade at your right hand. The sun shall not strike you by day, nor the moon by night. The Lord will keep you from all evil; he will keep your life. The Lord will keep your going out and your coming in from this time on and forevermore.

❖ ❖ ❖

As youth we recoil at the notion of needing a keeper. Aging adults recoil at the notion of assisted living. Everyone in between who is loaded with responsibilities thinks being taken care of sounds pretty good. The fact of the matter is that we do need a keeper. We need to know that in a world that spins out of our control that someone is doing more than watching with amusement as if we were the latest sensation on an internet video. The kind of watching our Lord does is active, compassionate and steadfast. In every sense of the word, He is a keeper.

❖ ❖ ❖

Precious Lord, hold us in the palm of your hand and love us into our lives. Amen.

MARCH ◆ 7

Romans 4:6-8
So also David speaks of the blessedness of those to whom God reckons righteousness apart from works: "Blessed are those whose iniquities are forgiven, and whose sins are covered; blessed is the one against whom the Lord will not reckon sin."

❖   ❖   ❖

In the American south, the word "reckon" means "thinking" usually accompanied by scratching one's scalp as if to stimulate cerebral matter into greater activity. "I reckon that will get us in a heap-a-trouble." It is a wonder that God does not bust a gut laughing at our goofy, childlike way of moving through our world. But we make God cry as much as we make him laugh as we continue to sin against him, one another and ourselves. When God reckons, he is considering a way in which the law which shapes our relationships still stands but our sinfulness is forgiven. Christ is the result of all God's reckoning for our sake.

❖   ❖   ❖

Holy God, your grace gives us the freedom to move beyond the prison of our own thinking. Amen.

MARCH ◆ 8

John 3:16-17
For God so loved the world that he gave his only Son, so that everyone who believes in him may not perish but may have eternal life. Indeed, God did not send the Son into the world to condemn the world, but in order that the world might be saved through him.

❖ ❖ ❖

Gospel in a nutshell. That is what these verses have been called. So simple yet we still have difficulty wrapping our heads around the magnitude of it. Not a week goes by when I don't hear of folks both within our community of faith and outside of it using the words of God like a hammer. Some make salvation a bargaining chip and do things to one another in the name of God that are light years removed from "God so loved the world..." Every once in a while, someone really gets it...and those moments shine like the sun.

❖ ❖ ❖

Lord God, we stand in awe of your amazing grace. Amen.

MARCH ◆ 9

John 4:6
Jesus, tired out by his journey, was sitting by the well.

❖   ❖   ❖

In the early years of the Christian faith, there were those who believed that Jesus was truly God but not human. When difficulties arise in matters of faith sometimes those who mean well seek to remove the obstacle, but in the process often harm the whole. If Jesus was not truly human then he might not have felt hunger or pain. The thorns pressed onto his head would not hurt like it would us. The cross was just a passage and not a real death. But those, like John, who traveled with Jesus witnessed his hunger and his agony. We need a God who is God. We need a God who is bigger than we can imagine, greater in wisdom and justice than anything we can create. We also need a God who understands a sleepless night, a blister, a broken heart. Such a God may be too big for us to wrap our heads around and believe. We need a God small enough to understand our weariness and big enough to hold the world while we sleep.

❖   ❖   ❖

Lord God, Thank you for being all that you are so that we can be all that you created us to be. Amen.

MARCH ◆ 10

Exodus 17:3-6
But the people thirsted there for water; and the people complained against Moses and said, "Why did you bring us out of Egypt, to kill us and our children and livestock with thirst?" So Moses cried out to the Lord, "What shall I do with this people? They are almost ready to stone me." The Lord said to Moses, "Go on ahead of the people, and take some of the elders of Israel with you; take in your hand the staff with which you struck the Nile, and go. I will be standing there in front of you on the rock at Horeb. Strike the rock, and water will come out of it, so that the people may drink." Moses did so, in the sight of the elders of Israel.

❖   ❖   ❖

Great leadership is more than just taking control and making good decisions. Leading so that others are given power and authority and share in the trust and respect that is built is a much more difficult thing. One of the best leaders I have known said that truly great leadership is when all the people can say, "Look what we have done together." God chose to work with Moses and chose to teach him a style of leadership that involved sharing the tasks and the authority. Moses had the window of opportunity to claim the glory for himself but he didn't. The Lord had helped Moses work through the problems of a thirsty and grumbly people in such a way that Moses' authority remained intact. We would be wise to work with one another with the same humility and encouragement.

❖   ❖   ❖

Holy God, may we lead with your wisdom and follow where you go. Amen.

MARCH ♦ 11

Psalm 95:1-4
O come, let us sing to the Lord; let us make a joyful noise to the rock of our salvation! Let us come into his presence with thanksgiving; let us make a joyful noise to him with songs of praise! For the Lord is a great God, and a great King above all gods. In his hand are the depths of the earth; the heights of the mountains are his also.

❖ ❖ ❖

The psalmist pulls us into worship like reluctant children kicking and screaming. "Say Please." "Say Thank you." We learn manners with a certain unwillingness, because it is simply easier to take what we want or receive what we need without any further words on our part. The music of healthy relationships has lyrics. By learning the song, we learn the language of gratitude. As we grow, those words become a way of life generated by a grateful heart. The "thank you" surfaces effortlessly. No matter where the words generate, God is still present to receive our childlike thanks. God always deserves our thanks and praise.

❖ ❖ ❖

Holy God, in all ways and for all purposes, we give you thanks. Amen.

MARCH ◆ 12

Romans 5:1-5
Therefore, since we are justified by faith, we have peace with God through our Lord Jesus Christ, through whom we have obtained access to this grace in which we stand; and we boast in our hope of sharing the glory of God. And not only that, but we also boast in our sufferings, knowing that suffering produces endurance, and endurance produces character, and character produces hope, and hope does not disappoint us, because God's love has been poured into our hearts through the Holy Spirit that has been given to us.

❖ ❖ ❖

I read a recent article that expressed concern that our culture is so focused on the issue of happiness that we are not dealing in a healthy way with the other emotions that shape our character. It is said that peace is not the absence of struggle but the presence of love. The scriptures are laced with songs of lament, frustration and fear. Throughout the story of God and God's people, however, there is the genuine source of meaning and hope that lies deeply in who God is to us. Our sadness is not to be denied or masked but surrounded with the power of the Holy Spirit alive in our lives. We cannot always remove the source of our sadness but we can be shielded from its power to steal our lives. Real joy comes not as a mental exercise but as a gift of the Spirit.

❖ ❖ ❖

Lord God, may we be open to the truth of our days and the power of your presence poured out for us. Amen.

MARCH ◆ 13

John 4:10-11
Jesus answered her, "If you knew the gift of God, and who it is that is saying to you, 'Give me a drink,' you would have asked him, and he would have given you living water." The woman said to him, "Sir, you have no bucket, and the well is deep. Where do you get that living water?

❖ ❖ ❖

"The Bucket List" came to fame in a Jack Nicholson movie. The premise of the movie is a couple of guys doing the things on a list that they would like to do before they "kicked the bucket." The bucket list that Jesus offers to the woman at the well is a different one. Jesus offers forgiveness and a promise of a new life. On the cross, Jesus dies for the sake of the world so that we could measure of our lives differently. Our lives don't have to be measured in a list of self-serving events - places we have seen and things we have done – to give us meaning and fullness. The only urgency that we face is that today there are those who need justice, kindness, forgiveness, and hope....there is no more important work to do before we enter into eternal life, than those who need the power of living water right now.

❖ ❖ ❖

Holy God, help us to receive your forgiveness and live a life that honors the gift. Amen.

MARCH ◆ 14

Jeremiah 31: 34
For I will forgive their iniquity, and remember their sin no more.

❖   ❖   ❖

One of the most important characteristics of God is that God chooses to forget. The fact that God can choose to forget in and of itself is an indication of God's divine power. Willfully forgetting a wrong done to us is simply beyond our power and even our comprehension. We are likely to say we forgive but cannot forget. Often we are not giving much more than lip-service to forgiveness. Forgiveness is always costly. Whether we need it ourselves or we need to offer it to someone else, the price of forgiveness is always the same & it is the life of God's Son. When we ask for forgiveness we are asking that Christ's death be applied to our account. When we give forgiveness, we are willing to accept Christ's death for the wrong done to us. Though the memory of the wrong still may linger in our heads, the power of it has disappeared in the cross. Forgiving and forgetting is not as complicated as we seem to make it. We just need to trust God with the forgetting part and concentrate on the true meaning of forgiveness.

❖   ❖   ❖

Merciful Lord, Forgive us as we have been forgiven. Amen.

MARCH ◆ 15

I Samuel 16:7
But the Lord said to Samuel, "Do not look on his appearance or on the height of his stature, because I have rejected him; for the Lord does not see as mortals see; they look on the outward appearance, but the Lord looks on the heart."

❖ ❖ ❖

In an election of political officials, public relations advisors know how important appearances are. I would hope people don't make crucial voting decisions based on surface impressions, but the reality is we do. The higher the office the less it seems to be about substance and the more about how the candidates are shaped and crafted by advisors for public consumption. The Lord consistently called those to leadership who may well have been rejected by those choosing leaders by human standards. Samuel would eventually be led by God to consider the young, harp-playing shepherd boy David as the king of Israel. Later in scriptures God would choose a short, ugly old Jewish man to become Paul - the first Christian missionary and the proclaimer of the Gospel to the Gentiles. May God bless us with the ability to see one another as God sees us.

❖ ❖ ❖

Holy God, Grant us the power to see beyond the surface to the heart and lift up those who will lead with depth of character. Amen.

MARCH ◆ 16

Psalm 32:3-5
While I kept silence, my body wasted away through my groaning all day long. For day and night your hand was heavy upon me; my strength was dried up as by the heat of summer. Then I acknowledged my sin to you, and I did not hide my iniquity; I said, "I will confess my transgressions to the Lord," and you forgave the guilt of my sin.

❖ ❖ ❖

Guilt is a boa constrictor that slithers deceptively up our legs and torso without putting the full weight of itself on us until it is across our shoulders. For a moment, we think we can hold it but then it starts to get heavy and then it starts to encircle our chest and our neck. It gives us breath to struggle but little else. It is in no hurry to destroy us but destroy us it will. Confession is the only way to release its death-dealing grip on us. The name of Jesus charms the deadliest of snakes.

❖ ❖ ❖

Holy God, help us to speak quickly our confession so that we do not waste the gift of time on the burden of guilt. Amen.

MARCH ◆ 17

Ephesians 5:10-14
Try to find out what is pleasing to the Lord. Take no part in the unfruitful works of darkness, but instead expose them. For it is shameful even to mention what such people do secretly; but everything exposed by the light becomes visible, for everything that becomes visible is light. Therefore it says, "Sleeper, awake! Rise from the dead, and Christ will shine on you."

❖ ❖ ❖

Our lives are filled with shadows, dark space, shut doors, unspoken ill will and twisted desires. We try to lead two lives - one in the dark and one in the light. The tension of our public and private selves takes its toll and we find ourselves not alone in the dark but in the company of guilt and shame. The darkness snacks on our bones. The Good News of God in Jesus Christ is that even though the light which shines on us stings at first, it brings us back into the company of the one who offered himself as a feast to save us from ourselves.

❖ ❖ ❖

Holy God, coax us out the dark and into the light of your grace. Amen.

MARCH ◆ 18

John 9:39-41
Jesus said, "I came into this world for judgment so that those who do not see may see, and those who do see may become blind." Some of the Pharisees near him heard this and said to him, "Surely we are not blind, are we?" Jesus said to them, "If you were blind, you would not have sin. But now that you say, 'We see,' your sin remains.

❖   ❖   ❖

On my 50th birthday, I had a conversation with a person who was well over 50. He said that I would love being 50 because "you have arrived - now you are wise and you don't have to listen to anyone else." There was a little tongue-in-cheek in the comment but only a little. A notably wiser fellow told me that "we die as we live." If we are arrogant, difficult, self-centered people then we are more so as we grow older and face our deaths. On his death bed, Martin Luther said, "we are sinners, it is true." As painful as my sinfulness and short-comings are to face, especially on a daily basis, I would rather live by the grace of God in the truth of my sin than by my own wit and wisdom inside a lie.

❖   ❖   ❖

Make us wise enough to know your will, O Lord, and strong enough to admit our sin. Amen.

MARCH ◆ 19

John 11:19
And many of the Jews had come to Martha and Mary to console them about their brother.

❖   ❖   ❖

"I don't know what to say." Those words are probably among the most frequently uttered at a funeral. In the presence of someone in emotional pain, we are often at a loss for words. We know from our own experience or just instinctively that whatever words we say will fall uselessly to the floor like dull arrows striking an impenetrable target. We fumble with statements that confess how we feel as if to let the person know that we stand on the edge of their ocean of pain with our toes in the water and feel the numbing cold. At worst, we say something truly dumb and walk away flogging ourselves for our insensitivity. The most powerful consolation we can offer is simply our presence. Words will fail. Presence sends a message beyond the words that cannot touch a broken heart. The Jews gathered to console Mary and Martha in their pain. But in the wings, we know there is One whose presence will make all the difference.

❖   ❖   ❖

Lord, May we know the consolation of your love and extend that loving presence to others. Amen.

MARCH ◆ 20

Luke 13:34-35
Jerusalem, Jerusalem, the city that kills the prophets and stones those who are sent to it! How often have I desired to gather your children together as a hen gathers her brood under her wings, and you were not willing! See, your house is left to you. And I tell you, you will not see me until the time comes when you say, 'Blessed is the one who comes in the name of the Lord.'"

❖ ❖ ❖

There is a Peanuts cartoon in which Lucy builds a snowman then destroys it then builds it again over and over. In the last frame, she said, "I am caught between the desire to create and demolish." Jerusalem had a long history of creation and demolition. The great temple of David was located there. The city had also known more than a few battles that leveled it. The people were defensive but also deeply critical and destructive. Some did not recognize the hope for a new future in the person of Jesus. They knew they could rebuild a city, but they could not rebuild a man after he was killed. That is the wonder of Easter and the marvel of God's grace. The time for demolition has ended. The new creation has come.

❖ ❖ ❖

Holy God, In the midst of our patterns of building one another up and tearing each other down, help us to see our salvation in your Son. Amen.

MARCH ◆ 21

Psalm 126:2
Then our mouth was filled with laughter, and our tongue with shouts of joy; then it was said among the nations, "The Lord has done great things for them."

❖ ❖ ❖

Laughter is the first baby step of faith and the dance music for the journey. The lyrics of laugher sing, "It sounds too good to be true, but there is a part of me that truly hopes it is." Throughout the struggles and stresses of an average day, there is the possibility of laughter that lingers in the air. There are those people who know how to generate a laugh and those who recognize a laughable thought when they hear it. Fueled by the grace of God like a spring of water deep within us, our laughter overflows. Despair and injustice still exist but the music of laughter, even in the distance, says that God is near.

❖ ❖ ❖

Fill us to overflowing, Lord, with your holy laughter. Amen.

MARCH ◆ 22

Isaiah 55:3,6,10-11
Incline your ear, and come to me; listen, so that you may live. I will make with you an everlasting covenant, my steadfast, sure love for David. ....Seek the Lord while he may be found, call upon him while he is near..... For as the rain and the snow come down from heaven, and do not return there until they have watered the earth, making it bring forth and sprout, giving seed to the sower and bread to the eater, so shall my word be that goes out from my mouth; it shall not return to me empty, but it shall accomplish that which I purpose, and succeed in the thing for which I sent it.

❖ ❖ ❖

I have a friend who literally inclines her ear to her children when they are standing or sitting by her side. With a simple tip of her head, she leans away from the noise around her to listen to her kids. She does the same thing in her relationship with God. I have another friend this week who has spent years inclining his ear to God and has now discovered his passion and mission in his vocational life. God does speak when we listen....his word does go forth and never comes back empty. We live our lives tipping our heads in God's direction and we will not be disappointed.

❖ ❖ ❖

Holy God, speak...your servants listen. Amen.

MARCH ◆ 23

Psalm 63
O God, you are my God, I seek you, my soul thirsts for you; my flesh faints for you, as in a dry and weary land where there is no water. So I have looked upon you in the sanctuary, beholding your power and glory. Because your steadfast love is better than life, my lips will praise you. So I will bless you as long as I live; I will lift up my hands and call on your name.

❖ ❖ ❖

Staying hydrated is important for health. We don't drink enough water during the day and our bodies react. The problem is often that we don't notice the sensation of thirst until we are well and truly dehydrated. We need to drink even when we are not thirsty. We are created for a relationship with God and we do get thirsty for it. We may choose to ignore it or try to satisfy the thirst with other things. We crawl to God often as last resort, but even first response to a crisis is not soon enough for good faith health. A relationship with God is not a first aid kit that we pull from the shelf occasionally but the air we breathe, the water we drink, the living stuff of which we are made.

❖ ❖ ❖

Holy God, may we be so aware of your presence today that you are in our breathing and our every thought. Amen.

MARCH ◆ 24

I Corinthians 10:13-17
No testing has overtaken you that is not common to everyone. God is faithful, and he will not let you be tested beyond your strength, but with the testing he will also provide the way out so that you may be able to endure it. Therefore, my dear friends, flee from the worship of idols. I speak as to sensible people; judge for yourselves what I say. The cup of blessing that we bless, is it not a sharing in the blood of Christ? The bread that we break, is it not a sharing in the body of Christ? Because there is one bread, we who are many are one body, for we all partake of the one bread.

❖ ❖ ❖

The discipline of a fast or giving up something up for a period of time is to help us see that our desires are not masters over us. For a brief time, we can tune out the desire that seems to have a hold on us and put it aside as if to say, "Sit, stay...you are not the boss of me." Nevertheless, our lives are a multitude of burdens to bear, temptations to resist - not the least of which is simply being selfish. God's word is constantly sounding to move us in his direction and turning us inside out. We discover again what we need and who we need on our journey. We discover again what we can leave at the side of the road.

❖ ❖ ❖

Precious Lord, grant us your strength to be greater together than we could ever be alone. Amen.

MARCH ◆ 25

Psalm 119:58-60
I implore your favor with all my heart; be gracious to me according to your promise. When I think of your ways, I turn my feet to your decrees; I hurry and do not delay to keep your commandments.

❖   ❖   ❖

I was having a conversation with a friend. We were talking about the difference between those people whose faith vibrates in everything they do compared to folks who just seem to be going through the motions. I recalled the last scene in the movie, "When Harry met Sally" where Harry is walking alone, lost and empty until he suddenly figures out what he really wants in his life. He starts to run several city blocks to the party Sally is attending. He arrives, not appropriately dressed for the formal party but runs to find Sally. The conversation goes back and forth with a frustrated and confused Sally asking Harry "Why are you doing this?" Harry says, "Because when you figure out that you want to spend the rest of your life with someone you want that life to start now." Our relationship with God is often like a romance where we push and pull and dance around each other and play games. We even break up and try to see who else is out there - what options do we have. There is a moment when it occurs to us that Jesus is the One. He offers the best deal in the world. When we turn our feet and run toward Jesus, we experience the exhilaration of a new life starting right now.

❖   ❖   ❖

Precious Lord, right now we turn toward you. Amen.

MARCH ◆ 26

Isaiah 43:18-19
Do not remember the former things, or consider the things of old. I am about to do a new thing; now it springs forth, do you not perceive it? I will make a way in the wilderness and rivers in the desert.

❖   ❖   ❖

When I traveled to Germany, I discovered how truly young the United States is. Germany's history goes so much deeper. I could sit on a step or lean against a wall or walk on a street that was centuries older than anything in the United States. There are plenty of "former things" to remember and old things worth remembering. It is also important to live in the present and dream of the future. We are the past that someone will reflect upon but they like us are called into each new day and to the future that beckons.

❖   ❖   ❖

Holy God, we give you thanks for our rich roots and those who have faithfully brought your Good News to each generation. Amen.

MARCH ◆ 27

Philippians 3:7-8
Yet whatever gains I had, these I have come to regard as loss because of Christ. More than that, I regard everything as loss because of the surpassing value of knowing Christ Jesus my Lord.

❖ ❖ ❖

I had a conversation with an old friend with whom I was catching up on family events. As he recounted the story of his son's wedding, he stopped and said how proud he was of his daughter-in-law because of her response in the midst of wedding planning when 9/11 happened. She wrote a story that appeared in the city paper about how in the blink of an eye she went from stressing about the color of napkins to being grateful for her life and her loved ones. If the ceremony happened in a living room, she would have been thrilled. That is what enormous tragedies do to us. They put our lives in perspective. We suddenly remember what is truly important. The cross of Christ is a great tragedy and a great hope if we are paying attention.

❖ ❖ ❖

Holy God, grant us the wisdom to see clearly what is important. Amen.

MARCH ◆ 28

Philippians 3:10-14
I want to know Christ and the power of his resurrection and the sharing of his sufferings by becoming like him in his death, if somehow I may attain the resurrection from the dead. Not that I have already obtained this or have already reached the goal; but I press on to make it my own, because Christ Jesus has made me his own. Beloved, I do not consider that I have made it my own; but this one thing I do: forgetting what lies behind and straining forward to what lies ahead, I press on toward the goal for the prize of the heavenly call of God in Christ Jesus.

❖   ❖   ❖

There is a something transcendent about knowing another person so well that a light touch on an arm or a brief glance in the eyes is an understanding that strikes cords of shared laughter or pain. It is a blessed thing to know and to be known. We have been given through word and sacraments an opportunity to know and to be known by the Creator of the Universe, the Master Designer, the Living God. What could we wish for our beloved ones that is greater that the knowledge of God? I knew of a person who had no goals and feared that God was finished with him. Apostle Paul, even as he stared at the end of his earthly life, could say with confidence that he still had more to do....that he sought to know Christ. It isn't a distraction from our lives....Christ is our lives.

❖   ❖   ❖

Holy God, I want to know you. I want to see your face and love as you love. Amen.

MARCH ◆ 29

John 12:3-6
Mary took a pound of costly perfume made of pure nard, anointed Jesus' feet, and wiped them with her hair. The house was filled with the fragrance of the perfume. But Judas Iscariot, one of his disciples (the one who was about to betray him), said, "Why was this perfume not sold for three hundred denarii and the money given to the poor?" (He said this not because he cared about the poor, but because he was a thief; he kept the common purse and used to steal what was put into it.)

❖ ❖ ❖

Judas criticizes Jesus. John makes sure that we know that Judas was concerned about himself. Jesus responded by saying the poor they would always have but they would not always have Jesus. Judas had the kind of poverty like a sink hole that never gets satisfied and gobbles more. We know people like this. They criticize. They are the squeaky wheels that always get attention. They get what they want and then want more and blame others for the negative atmosphere. They move through their world oblivious to the destruction and harm they cause. Other disciples would betray Jesus but in the self-awareness of their sin and belief in the power of Christ's forgiveness, they remained in the relationship with Christ and became the foundation for the Church...flawed, messy, imperfect and yet the Body of Christ alive today.

❖ ❖ ❖

Holy God, help us not to be afraid to face our own sin, embrace forgiveness and witness to the world of your mercy. Amen.

MARCH ◆ 30

I John 1:3-4
We declare to you what we have seen and heard so that you also may have fellowship with us; and truly our fellowship is with the Father and with his Son Jesus Christ. We are writing these things so that our joy may be complete.

❖ ❖ ❖

I have always been captivated by these verses because they seem to reach through a portal in time and grab me by ears as if to point my face at the ancient writer. Through this time window, the eye witnesses of the resurrection make eye contact. They speak to us SO THAT we can stand with them in fellowship with Jesus Christ. As much as I appreciate those who value their genealogical roots, I am still more interested in the roots of my faith that was passed from one person to another through generations to invade my soul. Those are lineages only known by the Spirit of God and yet I know that they exist because I am a part of the fellowship that has seen and heard about Jesus Christ. The completion of the joy is in telling others what we have seen and heard.

❖ ❖ ❖

Risen Lord, bless be the tie that bind our hearts in Christian love. Amen.

MARCH ◆ 31

Psalm 31:9-12
Be gracious to me, O Lord, for I am in distress; my eye wastes away from grief, my soul and body also. For my life is spent with sorrow, and my years with sighing; my strength fails because of my misery, and my bones waste away. I am the scorn of all my adversaries, a horror to my neighbors, an object of dread to my acquaintances; those who see me in the street flee from me. I have passed out of mind like one who is dead; I have become like a broken vessel.

❖   ❖   ❖

We don't stand beside grief very well. We don't know what to say or do. We lean against doorways waiting for an exit opportunity. We are overwhelmed to watch deep pain so we linger briefly and make excuses and breathe again when we turn the car key grateful to have some distance from something we can't fix and fear ever knowing ourselves. We sigh a prayer of gratitude that we are not that one. We are the fickled crowd of Jerusalem. We are today's cowards. We claim our own burdens to bear and shoulder them as best we can in the dark. We convince ourselves it is the best we can do. Jesus understands. Incredibly, Jesus understands. And he who knew no sin or sorrow, comes to our door, sits in our living room, drinks in our loneliness and takes death on. Incredible.

❖   ❖   ❖

Holy God, be gracious to us and let us live. Amen.

APRIL ◆ 1

Philippians 2:12-13
Therefore, my beloved, just as you have always obeyed me, not only in my presence, but much more now in my absence, work out your own salvation with fear and trembling; for it is God who is at work in you, enabling you both to will and to work for his good pleasure.

❖ ❖ ❖

I read a story the other day about a little girl who was standing at the bathroom mirror with her mouth open saying, "Are you in there?" When a parent finally asked her what she was doing, she said that she had been told that God was at work in her and she wanted to see what he was doing. Though not always as simply as looking in a mirror, even still, we do have a God who chooses to be involved in our lives. He did not set the world to spinning and walk away. He continues to work in us for his good purposes. When we do look in the mirror we can say, "Yes, God is in there." We might also add, "What can I do for you today?"

❖ ❖ ❖

Holy God, may the words of our mouths and the work of our hands delight you. Amen.

April ◆ 2

Luke 22:42-44
"Father, if you are willing, remove this cup from me; yet, not my will but yours be done." Then an angel from heaven appeared to him and gave him strength. In his anguish he prayed more earnestly, and his sweat became like great drops of blood falling down on the ground.

❖ ❖ ❖

In this verse, there is something huge between the semi-colon after "me" and the word "yet." I want to know what happened inside Jesus' mind and heart between those two phrases. He doesn't want to die but obedience to his Father's will take precedence over his own will. That is huge. It is a step that humanity had not been able to take because of our sinfulness. Jesus takes it for us. God sends strength to meet the difficult time ahead. God has given us a savior so that we might live and we are given strength for the journey in a variety of ways, in angels unaware. Between the semi-colon and "yet," hangs the salvation of the world. And Jesus chose us. Thanks be to God.

❖ ❖ ❖

We, your Easter people, stand in the shadow of your suffering and death and follow you into our lives of service and love. Amen.

APRIL ◆ 3

Psalm 133:1
How very good and pleasant it is when kindred live together in unity!

❖   ❖   ❖

From the beginning of the history of the people of Israel, they were given a vision. The vision was that God would be their God and they would be God's people. They would be given a homeland and a legacy of family. They had moments when they saw that dream realized. Those moments were often short-lived, but even in the ashes of shattered dreams they were given again the vision of one people, one God, one home forever. The vision remains imbedded in the core of who we are as children of God. We long to be in unity with one another. We ache to have the tension and the walls that separate us torn down. Even when we cannot seem to reach out to each other still we press our noses to the window and hope. Emily Dickinson once wrote that "Hope is a thing of feathers that perches on the soul. It sings the tune without the words and never stops at all." God keeps teaching us how to sing the song that dreams of God's people together.

❖   ❖   ❖

Lord God, we praise your name and sing your song of hope and unity. Amen.

APRIL ◆ 4

John 20:27-29
Then he said to Thomas, "Put your finger here and see my hands. Reach out your hand and put it in my side. Do not doubt but believe." Thomas answered him, "My Lord and my God!" Jesus said to him, "Have you believed because you have seen me? Blessed are those who have not seen and yet have come to believe."

❖   ❖   ❖

It was an essay question on a seminary exam. What one piece of scripture convinces you that the resurrection of Christ is true? There were several testimonies in the New Testament but the five words of Thomas "My Lord and My God" won the day for me. Thomas stood in the shoes of every doubter that would ever be. He spoke for all of us who can sound like lions of the faith in one breath and stutter the next. He stood where all of us have stood when the way gets murky and the trials are overwhelming. Jesus reached a scarred hand to a pouting skeptic and invited us all back onto the path of faith and discipleship.

❖   ❖   ❖

Holy God, we are weak. You are strong. Hold us up when our faith and courage falters. Amen.

APRIL ◆ 5

Psalm 31:9-12
Be gracious to me, O Lord, for I am in distress; my eye wastes away from grief, my soul and body also. For my life is spent with sorrow, and my years with sighing; my strength fails because of my misery, and my bones waste away. I am the scorn of all my adversaries, a horror to my neighbors, an object of dread to my acquaintances; those who see me in the street flee from me. I have passed out of mind like one who is dead; I have become like a broken vessel.

❖   ❖   ❖

I had a college friend who grew weary of hearing me lament on my life. One day, she shooed me out of her dorm room with the words, "Oh, go read a psalm!" She was knowledgeable enough of the scriptures to know that many of the psalms were prayers of those whose lives were difficult but clung to their faith. At first, "Go read a psalm!" had the character of a blunt dismissal much like a physician saying, "Take two aspirin and call me in the morning." It was, however, what I needed. I have had some pitiful days in my life, but the psalmist always trumped me in two ways. Their troubles were much worse than mine and their faith was quicker to kick in than mine. Growth in this journey seems to have less to do with the magnitude of our troubles and more to do with how quickly we turn and trust the grace of God.

❖   ❖   ❖

Lord, may I be as quick to turn to you as you are to chase me around. Amen.

APRIL ◆ 6

Isaiah 61:4
They shall build up the ancient ruins, they shall raise up the former devastations; they shall repair the ruined cities, the devastations of many generations.

❖   ❖   ❖

The sign of hope for the people of Israel was the restoration of their holy city of Jerusalem. In particular the temple was the focal point of their history and hope. Through the years, their enemies knew that to destroy their temple would be to break their spirit and destroy their will to fight. Whether it be a sprig of new growth in the midst of devastation or a "Now Open Again" sign, we are lifted up by indications that life has returned. Those who hope with such vigor become themselves witnesses to a greater promise still to come - the fulfillment of God's Kingdom.

❖   ❖   ❖

Precious Lord, we who shuffle around with the wreck of our days, look to you for signs of a new day. Amen.

APRIL ◆ 7

John 11:25-26
Jesus said to her, "I am the resurrection and the life. Those who believe in me, even though they die, will live, and everyone who lives and believes in me will never die. Do you believe this?"

❖ ❖ ❖

These words carry in them the memory of too many graveside services. I have sent these words "I am the resurrection and the life" over coffin lids and bowed heads, through dewy cemetery grass and between silent gravestones. "Do you believe this?" strikes us like thunder, like a finger jammed against our chest. We know how fragile our memories are. We cannot hold our loved ones in our minds for long in the busy demands of the day. The memories sit on shelves inside albums waiting for a visit. God wanted more for us than just memories and the weight of whispered names. Do we believe that Jesus is the resurrection and the life? Staring into graves, we are called to look up at Jesus - scarred and alive.

❖ ❖ ❖

We believe, Lord, help our unbelief. Amen.

APRIL ◆ 8

Acts 1
26 And they cast lots for them, and the lot fell on Matthias; and he was added to the eleven apostles.

❖   ❖   ❖

After Judas betrayed Jesus and died, the ranks of the apostles were diminished and a replacement was needed. They nominated two, prayed for God's wisdom and voted. The twelve including the one who wasn't chosen would eventually scatter to parts of the known world to spread the Good News about Jesus. Some would go into relative obscurity but all were believed to have a hand in making Christ known. The baton continues to be passed. It is in our hands.

❖   ❖   ❖

Lord, may we hear your voice and answer your call. Amen.

APRIL ◆ 9

Isaiah 50:5-8
The Lord God has opened my ear, and I was not rebellious, I did not turn backward. I gave my back to those who struck me, and my cheeks to those who pulled out the beard; I did not hide my face from insult and spitting. The Lord God helps me; therefore I have not been disgraced; therefore I have set my face like flint, and I know that I shall not be put to shame; he who vindicates me is near.

❖ ❖ ❖

When we are the victims of some injustice, it isn't unusual that we vent our frustration and anger at one person who represents the pain for us. The original brokenness is compounded by our reaction. The cycle continues. A few people behave badly and the whole group with whom they are associated is blamed. It never ceases to surprise me that people still expect the church to operate on a plain higher than our sinfulness allows. We turn toward Jesus who broke the cycle of pain and revenge by receiving unjust punishment without retaliation, without taking his marbles and going home, without finding another scapegoat for his pain. First, the momentum of the cycle has to be stopped and then its direction needs to be changed. Jesus did both.

❖ ❖ ❖

Help us, O Lord, to trust your will and your ways. Amen.

APRIL ◆ 10

Psalm 31:24
Be strong, and let your heart take courage, all you who wait for the LORD.

❖   ❖   ❖

I have a little piece of artwork in my office which was made for me. It bears the words "Courage sings with or without words." Courage is a deserving way to describe those who are on the frontlines of real conflict where lives are threatened. Courage also deserves to be used to describe single parents getting through an average day. We may not know how to be courageous but we know, that in circumstances both dramatic and sublime, we are called to tough it out. When courage sings with or without words we begin to hear what God is up to in our lives.

❖   ❖   ❖

Help me, Lord, wait and sing even when I don't know the words. Amen.

APRIL ◆ 11

Philippians 2:13
Therefore, my beloved, just as you have always obeyed me, not only in my presence, but much more now in my absence, work out your own salvation with fear and trembling; for it is God who is at work in you, enabling you both to will and to work for his good pleasure.

❖ ❖ ❖

The phrase "work out your own salvation" often trips us when we read it. If our salvation is from God then what does it mean for us to work it out? "Working out" does not negate God's grace but only re-enforces our responsibility to live obediently and responsibly inside the relationship we have been given in Christ. To believe that God is at work in us accomplishing his purposes gives meaning to days that may seem to be filled with only empty chores, thankless tasks and frustrating conversations. God is giving us everything we need to make profound differences in the lives of the people around us. Salvation is a dynamic act of God moving through us for others.

❖ ❖ ❖

Holy God, use all of our gifts for your good purposes. Amen.

April ◆ 12

Matthew 26:33-35
Peter said to him, "Though all become deserters because of you, I will never desert you." Jesus said to him, "Truly I tell you, this very night, before the cock crows, you will deny me three times." Peter said to him, "Even though I must die with you, I will not deny you." And so said all the disciples.

❖   ❖   ❖

"Promises, promises...." It is a wonder that we want to make promises given our inability to keep them. We love it when people make promises to us. "I promise I will always be your friend." "I promise I will love you forever." "I promise I will care for you no matter what happens." The promises never start out empty. They start out filled with the desire to reassure in a way that we ourselves would want to be reassured. Peter thinks everything will be all right as long as he hangs in there with Jesus. Jesus knows that what promise Peter has to offer is not enough. Peter cannot keep his own promises. At crunch time, Jesus clung to his promise to be obedient to God. God kept his promise to send us a Savior. Because those promises were made and fulfilled, every promise we make is filled with possibility and hope.

❖   ❖   ❖

Thank you, Lord, for the promise of a Savior especially on the days when we don't think we need one. Amen.

APRIL ◆ 13

John 19:39
Nicodemus, who had at first come to Jesus by night, also came.

❖ ❖ ❖

Nicodemus was a man of shadows. We know little about him except for his faith struggles. He was a member of the group of Jewish leaders who were opposed to Jesus' teachings. But there was something about this Jesus that compelled Nicodemus to steal away from his colleagues and in the cover of darkness go to Jesus. He asked him questions that betrayed his hunger to believe and his doubt. Nicodemus disappeared into the night with more questions than when he came. And yet, here is Nicodemus again. Lurking in the shadows of the crucified Christ, offering the spices and things needed to prepare his body. Was it a gesture motivated by guilt or devotion or both? Perhaps Nicodemus was the first Good Friday worshiper. We stand with him in the shadows with our own guilt, our own devotion and something more. Hope.

❖ ❖ ❖

God of Hope, even in the finality of the death of your Son, you give us reason to believe in life. Amen.

APRIL ◆ 14

Acts 10:45
The circumcised believers who had come with Peter were astounded that the gift of the Holy Spirit had been poured out even on the Gentiles.

❖ ❖ ❖

One of the first crises that the early Church faced was the issue of what it meant to be a Christian. Things haven't changed much in a couple thousand years. We all have our own understanding of what it means, what it should look like. We use language like "that is not very Christian of you" and go so far as questioning each other's salvation. God's Spirit works as it wills. When we are considering who is included or not included inside God's mercy and grace, our deepest focus might well be on being grateful that it includes the likes of us.

❖ ❖ ❖

Holy God, forgive us when we level judgment on one another in your name. Amen.

APRIL ◆ 15

Isaiah 42:3-4
A bruised reed he will not break, and a smoldering wick he will not snuff out. In faithfulness he will bring forth justice; he will not falter or be discouraged till he establishes justice on earth. In his law the islands will put their hope.

❖   ❖   ❖

I had an elementary teacher who ruled her classroom with a voice that rode on music and a touch that could gentle a lion. She was relentless in her soft forcefulness. Later when I found myself in a teaching role, I envied her the calming command that she had in her classroom. Because of it learning had a chance to happen. Jesus accomplished his purposes in such a way that God was honored in every step, in every conversation. Sometime in our fervor and passion to accomplish a task we run over the people the task was intended to help. Sometimes the way in which we make decisions are as important as any decision that we make. God accomplishes his purposes without breaking our spirit to the point of destruction. God accomplishes his purposes with us and for us.

❖   ❖   ❖

Holy God, from beginning to end, you have thought of our best interest and greatest good. May we be as relentless in our desire to serve you. Amen.

APRIL ◆ 16

Psalm 71:17-19
O God, from my youth you have taught me, and I still proclaim your wondrous deeds. So even to old age and gray hairs, O God, do not forsake me, until I proclaim your might to all the generations to come. Your power and your righteousness, O God, reach the high heavens. You who have done great things, O God, who is like you?

❖ ❖ ❖

The older I get the more stories I have. The wiser I get I remember that not every story is worth telling. Jesus spent his last days with his beloved disciples telling them what he most wanted them to know - that God is real, true, active and alive - that God loved them beyond their imagination and the magnitude of their sin. Every generation needs to hear again from living witnesses that God is real. I question every day what really matters....what are the important decisions and conversations and what are empty exercises. From the beginning of the day to my last conscious thought and every breath in between, God, my Creator, Redeemer and Sustainer, is the most real and most honest story to tell.

❖ ❖ ❖

Grant me, O Lord, the courage to tell what I have seen and heard of your mighty deeds alive in my life. Amen.

April ◆ 17

Hebrews 12:1-3
Therefore, since we are surrounded by so great a cloud of witnesses, let us also lay aside every weight and the sin that clings so closely, and let us run with perseverance the race that is set before us, looking to Jesus the pioneer and perfecter of our faith, who for the sake of the joy that was set before him endured the cross, disregarding its shame, and has taken his seat at the right hand of the throne of God. Consider him who endured such hostility against himself from sinners, so that you may not grow weary or lose heart.

❖ ❖ ❖

The joy set before him. Imagine what it would be to discover that the joy that was set before Jesus to motivate him toward suffering and his own death was an image of you resting in peace in God's arms. It is humbling indeed to realize that the joy that was set before Jesus to motivate him to move toward the suffering and shame of the cross was an image of you and me. This would be humbling indeed. Given what God has done and continues to do in our lives, it is tragically petty of us when we cling to our grudges and stew in our dislikes and pout over our shortcomings. Just because we are claimed as children of God does not mean we don't need to grow up. There is much to do and many are needed and time isn't being wasted...lives are. The joy set before us is a race in which we all win.

❖ ❖ ❖

Holy God, kick us from the complacency of the sidelines and into the race for the sake of the world. Amen.

APRIL ◆ 18

Luke 23:42-43
Then he said, 'Jesus, remember me when you come into your kingdom.' He replied, 'Truly I tell you, today you will be with me in Paradise.'

❖ ❖ ❖

In the last dying breaths of a sinful man, a criminal recognized his own guilt and the innocence of Jesus. All that is left for him is the few minutes before his death. He casts all his hope on memory of the innocent man before him. Jesus' response to this man was more than the promise of remembrance. He says in essence, "today you are where I am and today you will be where I will be." The sinful man will be more than a good man's memory. He will be forgiven and free and he will recognize all that he was meant to be. Paradise may well be a place for all we know but it is more. It is where we will be face to face with love without having to squint the eyes of our hearts to see it.

❖ ❖ ❖

Precious Lord, remember me when you come into your kingdom. Amen.

APRIL ◆ 19

Acts 2:14
But Peter, standing with the eleven, raised his voice and addressed them, "Men of Judea and all who live in Jerusalem, let this be known to you, and listen to what I say.

❖ ❖ ❖

Between Jesus' death and Pentecost in Jerusalem was a span of about four weeks. During Jesus' death, Peter was the one hiding in the shadows and insisting he didn't know the man who he had just spent every day for the last four years. A little over a month later in Jerusalem, Peter is not only owning up to knowing him – he is speaking to thousands. The one who cowered and mumbled in fear is now standing with the other disciples to proclaim the Kingdom of God now come. Throughout the history of Christendom, there is no greater witness to the power of God than the testimony of a changed life. The message of Easter is that no one is hopeless. Life is full of change that is often unwelcome. Life is also full of change that is incredibly good and eternal.

❖ ❖ ❖

Holy God, death has been changed from powerful enemy to vanquished foe. Amen.

APRIL ◆ 20

Psalm 16:2
I say to the Lord, "You are my Lord; I have no good apart from you."

❖ ❖ ❖

I have met a lot of people who seem rather content to lead small lives. They carve out a tiny world. They set themselves no greater goals than getting through the day, earning the paycheck, limiting relationships to those who are willing to shrink themselves into their little worlds and not challenge it in any way. They are masters at ignoring God and just about everything and everyone else. Their lives have a simplicity to it that others may even envy. Inevitably the world outside of our control comes crashing our little parties. We have small worlds because we want control. We want control to be like God. We are terrible at it. God offers us a world with unlimited possibilities as long as we let him be God.

❖ ❖ ❖

Holy God, apart from you, we are nothing. Amen.

April ◆ 21

I Peter 1:6-7
In this you rejoice, even if now for a little while you have had to suffer various trials, so that the genuineness of your faith-being more precious than gold that, though perishable, is tested by fire-may be found to result in praise and glory and honor when Jesus Christ is revealed.

❖ ❖ ❖

The first century Church was faced with sufferings, persecution, and death for the sake of their faith. When they used words like "trial" or "sufferings" or "tested by fire," it was the real deal. I am regularly ashamed that I think trial or suffering has to do with the petty inconveniences that I encounter. Faith that is understood as the patience we receive to get through the frustration of not knowing what to make for dinner is faith that is seriously in need of some growing. There are real battles to be fought and won for Jesus' sake. We need to engage the fight with the real deal of what it means to believe in Jesus Christ and to be his faithful followers.

❖ ❖ ❖

Precious Lord, help us to recognize the real fight when we see it. Amen.

APRIL ◆ 22

John 20:26-28
A week later his disciples were again in the house, and Thomas was with them. Although the doors were shut, Jesus came and stood among them and said, "Peace be with you." Then he said to Thomas, "Put your finger here and see my hands. Reach out your hand and put it in my side. Do not doubt but believe." Thomas answered him, "My Lord and my God!"

❖ ❖ ❖

Thomas lives in infamy as one who doubts. He carries on his reputation the doubts of generations who understand him better than perhaps any other eye witness to the resurrection. The challenge for us is not in relating to Thomas' doubt which we do easily and readily. The challenge is relating to the faith that compelled him to say, "My Lord and my God!" Doubting is a part of what it means to be a Christian, but so is believing when a doubter tells us the truth.

❖ ❖ ❖

Holy God, I believe. Help my unbelief. Amen.

APRIL ◆ 23

John 21:5-6
Jesus said to them, "Children, you have no fish, have you?" They answered him, "No." He said to them, "Cast the net to the right side of the boat, and you will find some." So they cast it, and now they were not able to haul it in because there were so many fish.'

I am an "outside the box" kind of thinker. It doesn't mean that I don't appreciate the box. It doesn't mean I ignore the box. It does mean I start out in the box. If the box works, I try my best to let it be. If the box isn't working, then I am quick to bend the walls, poke windows, and as needed, to leap completely out of the box to try a new thing. The Church from the beginning was and is good at building boxes. When life got confusing and uncomfortable for the disciples, they went back to the box of fishing that was familiar to them. We tend to do that in the Church as well. Jesus invited the disciples first to fish in a little less familiar waters. It would be the prelude for inviting them to be "outside the boat" thinkers. We are followers of Jesus Christ because someone fished outside their box in our direction. So too, we are called.

❖ ❖ ❖

Holy God, make us restless to serve you. Amen.

April ◆ 24

I John 4:1
Do not believe every spirit, but test the spirits to see whether they are from God.

❖   ❖   ❖

Serving on a candidacy committee whose task is to work with those studying for professional ministry, we would ask the candidates about their internal and external sense of call. The internal call is their own personal understanding of their gifts and how they discern their call to God's people. The external call comes through the faithful voices of other Christians who know God and know that candidate and can affirm that they have gifts for ministry. It is the Church's way of "testing the spirit" so that those who are given the great responsibility of leadership are there not because of their individual voice but the Holy Spirit's call through the Body of Christ. Going into parish ministry is a big decision but every big decision we face can include testing the Spirit by listening to the truth inside of us and around us. Whose voice do we trust to tell us God's truth? When the stakes are high, we can and should take the time to discern God's truth as we participate in the Body of Christ.

❖   ❖   ❖

Holy God, in decisions big and small help us to hear your voice with clarity. Amen.

APRIL ◆ 25

John 10:27-28
My sheep hear my voice. I know them, and they follow me. I give them eternal life, and they will never perish. No one will snatch them out of my hand.

❖   ❖   ❖

You don't have to work too hard these days to find people who reject Christianity because Christians are so close-minded. It terms of our judgment of other people we are, certainly, guilty as charged. Next to those who don't believe in God and believe this life is all there is, a Christian is much more open-minded. We believe in possibility and life that goes on forever - that is quintessential open-mindedness. I imagine this life sometimes as a shadowy passage through a forest in which the light only penetrates in flashes and through translucent green leaves. When we lose our sense of direction, we may choose to move in the direction of a sound, especially a familiar sound. I imagine that I will clear the shadows one day and walk into a clearing that blows my mind and finds me forever home. I am open to other ideas because as we listen to Christ's voice, even in our shadowlands, our minds are being stretched with new possibilities. It beats sitting in a closed room with no windows any day.

❖   ❖   ❖

Holy God, open us up to all of your possibilities. Amen.

APRIL ◆ 26

Mark 11:29
Jesus said to them, "I will ask you one question; answer me, and I will tell you by what authority I do these things.

❖   ❖   ❖

There is a scene in the movie "Yentl" which takes place in a classroom of a Hebrew university. At first glance, it looks more like a cafeteria. There are tables jammed with students sitting across from one another. The room is alive with human voices. The rabbinical style of teaching is less lecture and more question and answer. Jesus was a rabbi who looked at every moment as a teaching opportunity. He confounded and challenged those around him by answering questions with questions. He often used questions to redirect people to higher purposes. Those who opposed Jesus used the weapons of their wisdom to plot his death. But God used even the events of the cross as a teaching moment for the world. There is something greater than death. God's answer to death is the power of his love.

❖   ❖   ❖

Lord God, teach us how we might be obedient to the law of love. Amen.

APRIL ◆ 27

Mark 12:10
Have you not read this scripture: The stone that the builders rejected has become the keystone.

❖   ❖   ❖

In a college community, I have seen relationships begin and often end on a regular basis. Roommate problems abound in the early years of college as students adjust to living with someone other than their own family. Dating becomes more serious as couples wonder if he or she might be "the one." Amidst the many solid relationships there is the wreckage of shattered ones. The heart continues to beat inside chests that feel heavy, weighed down with broken pieces. As the drama of Jesus' passion unfolds we witness a man being rejected by the wisest people of the community and even by his friends. Jesus understands what it means to be rejected by those who he loves the most. The sting of a whip on his skin would only confirm what he will feel in his heart. The new promise between God and God's people will be based on that which was rejected. From the broken pieces God will build a new world.

❖   ❖   ❖

Lord, forgive us for our rejection of your love and receive the offering of our broken hearts. Amen.

APRIL ◆ 28

Psalm 148:3-4
Praise him, sun and moon; praise him, all you shining stars! Praise him, you highest heavens, and you waters above the heavens!

❖ ❖ ❖

There are days, especially when working with youth, in which I feel like merchant of wonder. As amazed as I am by the technical gadgets that are second-nature to them, some of their muscles of amazement are atrophying. A tree, a sea of pea gravel in a playground, a grassy grove are undiscovered country within footsteps of our church's door. We walked and talked and spoke of types of prayer. We considered a tree like we would a masterpiece hanging in museum. We confessed our sins in the shifty gravel. We dreamed in a quiet grove and we waved at passing cars. We did it all in the name of the one who gave us this incredible space in which to live and wired us for wonder. The psalmist invites us to look again at a world charged with the grandeur of God.

❖ ❖ ❖

Great job, Lord! Amen.

APRIL ◆ 29

John 10:27-30
My sheep hear my voice. I know them, and they follow me. I give them eternal life, and they will never perish. No one will snatch them out of my hand. What my Father has given me is greater than all else, and no one can snatch it out of the Father's hand. The Father and I are one.'

❖ ❖ ❖

I've watched enough of the Animal Channel to know that mother animals and their young know the sound of each other's voice. Nevertheless, I am still amazed when child says, "Mom" in a roomful of mothers that the right one usually responds. How does a small child seem to be able to locate a parent in a forest of adult legs? They just do. They just do because they have to. They have no choice. They must. The ones who know the voice of the Savior are the ones who have known the sound of tears in the middle of the night. They are the ones who have felt lost in a forest of their own making. The ones who have known fear and pain that slices from the inside out. These know the voice of a shepherd because they have to. They have no choice. There is mercy and peace in God's care. God stands boldly between them and those who would feed on them. This shepherd is unique in that he is not only shepherd but a lamb as well. Those who need Jesus the most are the ones who recognize his voice because it sounds familiar, like one of their own.

❖ ❖ ❖

Lord God, continue to speak to us so that we will become familiar with your loving voice. Amen.

APRIL ◆ 30

Ezekiel 37:26-28
I will make a covenant of peace with them; it shall be an everlasting covenant with them; and I will bless them and multiply them, and will set my sanctuary among them for evermore. My dwelling-place shall be with them; and I will be their God, and they shall be my people. Then the nations shall know that I the Lord sanctify Israel, when my sanctuary is among them for evermore.

❖   ❖   ❖

The history of the people of God from ancient times to the present has been one of scattering and gathering. The scattering happened often after a united people behaved as if they no longer needed God. During the time of their scattering they developed a new appreciation for and a deep longing for home. God gathered his people again time after time. Though the times when the people were dispersed were both challenging and renewing, they were never forgotten. God always had their forwarding address. When the time was right, God called them to gather again. God called the people home. Sometimes God called them to the temple in Jerusalem or under wing of a solitary leader. God always reiterated the promise of the covenant: land, blessing, family, one God. In our scattered condition on the earth, we know what it is to long for home and to be one with each other and our God. It is a longing that gives us a glimpse of God's heart.

❖   ❖   ❖

Lord God, we, your scattered people, listen to your gathering cry and long for home. Amen.

MAY ◆ 1

Ezekiel 45:3
In the holy district you shall measure off a section in which shall be the sanctuary, the most holy place.

❖   ❖   ❖

T.S. Eliot spoke of love as being the "stillpoint of the turning world." When so little ever stays the same, when the children grow before our eyes, when the gods of busy schedule are thrown their daily sacrifices of our time, we need no reminder of a turning world. We do, however, need to find those places that hold the still, solid territories of the truth about who we are and who God is. The temple for the people of Israel was that irrefutable place to which they could go and believe that God was present. It is the holy space where the walls between the Kingdom here and the Kingdom not yet are so thin that one can almost see through them. The stillpoint is more than the stoppage of busy-ness, but a foothold from where we can glimpse the peaceful presence of God. It is that place where we can dare to press our palms on the fortress walls and feel a heart beating. With the gift of the Holy Spirit, Christ gave us the ability to make any space holy, any point in a turning world still, even if only for a moment.

❖   ❖   ❖

Lord God, grant us a quiet stillness in the constant turbulence of our days. Amen.

MAY ◆ 2

2 Timothy 4:13
When you come, bring the cloak that I left with Carpus at Troas, also the books, and above all the parchments.

❖   ❖   ❖

Paul was finishing up his letter to Timothy. It included a few greetings, information about colleagues, a warning about opponents and this minor detail about some items Paul wanted him to retrieve. I get frustrated with details. I get frustrated having to take precious time off from work for household chores. I get frustrated with people whose lives seem to be more consumed with details than what I consider more important. I get frustrated that when my own disregard for details sends me scrambling to meet a deadline or makes a task more energy-sapping than it ever needed to be. I doubt that Paul intended any profound Gospel truth woven inside these words requesting a cloak and some books and papers. Maybe it just makes me feel better today knowing that Paul still had laundry to do while he was doing the important stuff.

❖   ❖   ❖

Lord, comfort and guide us through the clutter of our days. Amen.

MAY ◆ 3

Jeremiah 50:19
I will restore Israel to its pasture, and it shall feed - its hunger shall be satisfied.

❖   ❖   ❖

Abraham Maslow, the great humanist, in his "Hierarchy of Needs" described levels of human need. The most basic of needs is physiological. In order to continue to be living, we need oxygen, food, water, protection from the severe elements. The most fundamental military strategy understands that an army travels on its stomach. Food is essential. If the food supply lines are cut off, then the enemy is weakened and vulnerable. God has always been attentive to the most basic human needs. God was even willing to listen for menu requests in the wilderness when the people tired of eating manna. During times of drought and famine, we know of a God who carefully attended to feeding the prophets so that they could continue to feed the people with hope. Israel would be fed. So too are we given that which we need most basically to thrive even as we continue to hunger for food and righteousness.

❖   ❖   ❖

Holy God, make us ever mindful of the food you give us every day. Amen.

MAY ◆ 4

Acts 8:35-36
Then Philip began to speak, and starting with this scripture, he proclaimed to him the good news about Jesus. As they were going along the road, they came to some water; and the eunuch said, "Look, here is water! What is to prevent me from being baptized?"

❖ ❖ ❖

Of rhetorical questions, this one of the Ethiopian man in this story is a big one. It is so big that I am even inclined to answer it. What is to prevent me from being baptized? NOTHING! There is nothing, absolutely nothing, nada, zip preventing us from being baptized. Water is readily available. Depending on your faith tradition, the amount of water may or may not be an issue. We are becoming more aware of the need for drinkable water in areas of our world. Nevertheless, water for baptism is at the ready. God's word and promise is never more than a breath away. Very often the obstacles to baptism are human ones. Everyone is free to come to water and receive this sacrament of a new life.

❖ ❖ ❖

Thanks, Lord, for chasing us and giving us the faith we need to splash around in our baptismal promises. Amen.

MAY ♦ 5

Psalm 67:1-2
May God be gracious to us and bless us and make his face to shine upon us, that your way may be known upon earth, your saving power among all nations.

❖   ❖   ❖

We expect grace. We need grace. We would wither and die without grace. We pray for God's grace and that his power will be known by everyone. God chooses to make his grace most known by calling us to love as we have been love. God chooses to make his grace known through people like us. That's a problem. People like us are not always champions of undeserved love. Grace is a difficult concept for us to wrap our heads around no matter how deeply we need it. We understand the freedom it grants us. But the power of grace is the free choice we have to show that grace to others. God in his grace changes the rules of our relationships. God's power is shown in how often we who are blessed can be a blessing for others.

❖   ❖   ❖

Holy God, may the grace you extend to us shine in us for the sake of others. Amen.

MAY ◆ 6

I John 4:7-8
Beloved, let us love one another, because love is from God; everyone who loves is born of God and knows God. Whoever does not love does not know God, for God is love.

❖ ❖ ❖

We do a little children's version of liturgy for our Early Learning Center's weekly chapel service. Before the Bible story for the day is told the children say, "The Holy Bible is God's book. Let's open it and see where God tells us he loves us. He loves you and he loves me." I told the story today of Phillip in Acts who encounters a fellow who needs help understanding the scriptures and the bottom line of the story was what the little pre-school children already know - the Bible is a book about love. The love in scriptures is roll-up-your-sleeves, it is going to be a bumpy ride, hang-on for dear life kind of love. The message of God's Word is powerfully simple. God sent his Son so that the power of love could be released on the world in and through us.

❖ ❖ ❖

Holy God, for your Word, your Son, your grace we give you thanks and pray that we will learn to love as you love us. Amen.

MAY ◆ 7

Ezekiel 37:27
My dwelling place shall be with them; and I will be their God, and they shall be my people.

❖   ❖   ❖

The history of the people of God from ancient times to the present has been one of scattering and gathering. The scattering happened often after a united people behaved as if they no longer needed God. During the time of their scattering, they developed a new appreciation and a deep longing for home. God gathered his people again time after time. Though the times when the people were dispersed were both challenging and renewing, they were never out of God's mind. God always had their forwarding address. And when the time was right, God called them to gather again. God called the people home. In our scattered condition on the earth, we know what it is to long for home and to be one with each other and our God. It is a longing that gives us a glimpse of God's heart.

❖   ❖   ❖

Lord God, we, your scattered people, listen to your gathering cry and long for home. Amen.

MAY ◆ 8

I Peter 1:22-23
Now that you have purified your souls by your obedience to the truth so that you have genuine mutual love, love one another deeply from the heart. You have been born anew, not of perishable but of imperishable seed, through the living and enduring word of God.

❖ ❖ ❖

When life gets complicated and cluttered, we are encouraged by the word of God to attend to simple truth and reclaim our purpose to love. We continue to sweat the small things and stew over matters beyond our control. We grumble about how other people move through their lives and their responsibilities. Time and again we are called back into remembering the world that God rules now and forever. We are along for the ride. All that is asked of us is that we love those who are on the journey with us.

❖ ❖ ❖

Holy God, for the ride of our lives into the joy of your everlasting Kingdom we give you thanks. Amen.

MAY ◆ 9

Luke 24:45-47
Then he opened their minds to understand the scriptures, and he said to them, "Thus it is written, that the Messiah is to suffer and to rise from the dead on the third day, and that repentance and forgiveness of sins is to be proclaimed in his name to all nations, beginning from Jerusalem. You are witnesses of these things.

❖ ❖ ❖

The pony express riders of the early American west rode alone with urgency through inclement weather, darkness, insecure territory to do what we can now do with a finger on a packet of handheld technology. Communication methods have changed dramatically through the centuries but the method of communicating the Good News of God in Jesus Christ remains the same. It is one beggar telling another beggar how to find bread. We carry the news of Christ's redemption in our bodies and we pull them through our hearts, lungs, through voice boxes, teeth and tongue, tears and eyes to tell others what we have seen and heard. Jesus is alive. I have seen him.

❖ ❖ ❖

Holy God, stir us to tell others what we believe about your Son. Amen.

MAY ◆ 10

Genesis 15:6
And he believed the LORD; and the LORD reckoned it to him as righteousness.

❖ ❖ ❖

Compared to Abram, we have a whole boatload of history with the Lord. We have the rest of the Bible and the story of the early Church and the witness of millions who have testified that God has kept his promises. Abram could plunge his hands into the pockets of his history with God and find less than lint. And yet, at God's word of promise, Abram left to go to a far country. Along the way, Abram showed that he was more accustomed to taking care of himself and his own family than trusting anyone else. Abram's journey of faith was not so smooth, but what faith he had compelled him to move in God's direction. Those baby steps were enough for God to call Abram a righteous man. To each new life God renews his promises. Armed with a history of God's faithfulness to people like Abram for thousands of years, we who move in baby steps of faith in God's direction can be confident of God's applause and delight even when we feel ourselves like less than lint.

❖ ❖ ❖

Holy God, receive our steps of faith toward to you today. Amen.

MAY ◆ 11

Acts 2:42-45
They devoted themselves to the apostles' teaching and fellowship, to the breaking of bread and the prayers. Awe came upon everyone, because many wonders and signs were being done by the apostles. All who believed were together and had all things in common; they would sell their possessions and goods and distribute the proceeds to all, as any had need.

❖   ❖   ❖

The kind of generosity displayed by the community of early Christians was compelling. We can temper it with the notions that they had been eyewitnesses to the resurrection or, at least, been in the presence of eye witnesses. We could explain it by saying they were expecting Christ's imminent return and had no thought of the future. We could blame them for foolishness because their spontaneous generosity only created a new poor in Jerusalem that would need the generosity of others to survive. All those excuses make us feel less guilty when we are guarded and limited in our giving. Our discipleship may not yet be at that level of generous stewardship. No matter where we are, we can take note of the fact that the Good News of Jesus Christ compelled them to live with a new standard and a new freedom. It is that news that continues to call us to a greater level of love and life as we know it.

❖   ❖   ❖

Captivate us with your word, O Lord, and lead us to a generous heart. Amen.

MAY ◆ 12

Revelation 21:22-25
I saw no temple in the city, for its temple is the Lord God the Almighty and the Lamb. And the city has no need of sun or moon to shine on it, for the glory of God is its light, and its lamp is the Lamb. The nations will walk by its light, and the kings of the earth will bring their glory into it. Its gates will never be shut by day—and there will be no night there.

❖   ❖   ❖

The church building of my growing up years was built around the time of the Revolutionary War. The interior was dark wood and heavy crimson velvet curtains. It looked and felt like the inside of a hearse. The steeple started to lean beyond repair and the building was torn down and replaced with a new one. The new sanctuary was white and windowed, bright and soaring. I wasn't used to it. It almost hurt my eyes after years of funeral home decor. As much as it was unfamiliar to me, it was still intoxicating with its light and I could not even imagine the darkness. We should fling wide our doors and file our bricks to translucency and prepare for the Kingdom of God.

❖   ❖   ❖

Holy God, bring on the light. Amen.

MAY ◆ 13

I Peter 2:24-25
He himself bore our sins in his body on the cross, so that, free from sins, we might live for righteousness; by his wounds you have been healed. For you were going astray like sheep, but now you have returned to the shepherd and guardian of your souls.

❖ ❖ ❖

We carry guilt around. That is a given. We sin and we know we sin and we feel guilty about it. The guilt snacks on our bones and drools on our spirit and sucks the life out of us. We invite it to dine on us because we can't believe that the cross of Jesus Christ is big enough to grant us forgiveness. We aren't given grace because we deserve it but because we are loved. We have difficulty imagining that kind of love extended in our direction given what we know about ourselves. But we are called every day to arise again to the Great Miracle that God knows everything about us and loves us nonetheless. We are free. Free for a reason - to bring the Good News of grace to a chewed up world.

❖ ❖ ❖

Holy God, help us to bring the burden of our guilt to the cross and leave it there. Amen.

MAY ◆ 14

Psalm 22:30-31
Posterity will serve him; future generations will be told about the Lord, and proclaim his deliverance to a people yet unborn, saying that he has done it.

❖   ❖   ❖

I am amused with the studies that promote the idea that children in the womb can begin to learn by listening to music being played through the muffled wall of the mother's abdomen. Who am I to refute it? I do, however, reserve the right to snicker a little. Classical music is usually the music of choice assuming that it is the music most associated with fine breeding and intellect. Perhaps rap or rock will just lead them more quickly down the path of rebellion. Why not play lectures by Einstein or speeches by the great orators? In the end, we want our children to know, at the very least, the truest things that we know. For generations, the word has been passed from one tender child to another - "I know that my Redeemer lives. His name is Jesus and he loves you bigger than life."

❖   ❖   ❖

Holy God, let us lay hold of the truth that we know and sing it to next generation. Amen.

MAY ◆ 15

John 1:48
"Where did you get to know me?" Jesus answered, "I saw you under the fig tree..."

❖   ❖   ❖

An oft-repeated sentiment I hear during pre-marital counseling is that "He/she knows me, knows what I am thinking, can finish my sentences." In our most intimate relationships, trust is absolutely critical and fragile. Trust can be undergirded with a deep knowledge that is sown with benevolent purposes. To be known by one who we do not know or trust can be scary. To enter into a relationship with Jesus we encounter someone who knows us better than we do ourselves. If the fear of being discovered doesn't chase us away, we will find in Christ one whose motives are completely for us. To grow in the intimate knowledge of Jesus is to discover a loved one who enjoys filling in the blanks of our incomplete sentences.

❖   ❖   ❖

Holy God, help us not to be afraid of your intimate knowledge of who we are. Amen.

MAY ◆ 16

Acts 7:30-33
Now when forty years had passed, an angel appeared to him in the wilderness of Mount Sinai, in the flame of a burning bush. When Moses saw it, he was amazed at the sight; and as he approached to look, there came the voice of the Lord: 'I am the God of your ancestors, the God of Abraham, Isaac, and Jacob.' Moses began to tremble and did not dare to look. Then the Lord said to him, 'Take off the sandals from your feet, for the place where you are standing is holy ground.

❖ ❖ ❖

In a discussion group, we were talking about worship and what it means to be in the presence of God. We who plan worship services certainly hope that we create an opportunity for people to know, feel and reverence the presence of God. Some churches whip up the people with sermons that build to crescendos or with spirited music. Some offer time of meditative quiet and tender prayers. Whatever we feel or don't feel in the worship service, God makes himself present and available to us in his word and in communion. It may not have the drama of a burning bush. In a bit of bread and a sip of wine in the company of others we have an opportunity to press our noses against the place where the walls between the kingdom now and the kingdom yet to be are thin. Holy ground indeed.

❖ ❖ ❖

Lord God, until the time that all ground is once again holy, we praise your name and wait for your coming again. Amen.

MAY ◆ 17

Psalm 31:14-16
But I trust in you, O Lord; I say, "You are my God." My times are in your hand; deliver me from the hand of my enemies and persecutors. Let your face shine upon your servant; save me in your steadfast love.

❖   ❖   ❖

What comes before the "But I trust in you, O Lord" is a litany of awful things that were happening to the psalmist. Life in every way was miserable. Sometimes the pit is so dark and so deep. There appears to be no good options for escape we take a breath and fling ourselves into God's hands. *Letting go* and *letting God* are two of the most difficult and utterly necessary things we do. More often than not we exhaust ourselves before we finally release the strangle hold we have on our own lives. Whether we trust early or late, God saves - God shines - God loves.

❖   ❖   ❖

Holy God, out of the depths we cry to you trusting in your gracious love. Amen.

MAY ◆ 18

I Peter 2:4-5, 10
Come to him, a living stone, though rejected by mortals yet chosen and precious in God's sight, and like living stones, let yourselves be built into a spiritual house, to be a holy priesthood, to offer spiritual sacrifices acceptable to God through Jesus Christ. Once you were not a people, but now you are God's people; once you had not received mercy, but now you have received mercy.

❖   ❖   ❖

Groucho Marx said, "I don't want to belong to any club that would have me for a member." The issue of how church membership happens is a topic that often surfaces. Should the process for membership be quick and easy or slow and thorough? What should be required? At the same time, more church shoppers are simply asking, "Why join? If we attend and participate, what is the point of a membership process?" What benefit is there to membership when, in most churches, one cannot distinguish the members from non-members? As an organizational issue, there is no clean answer. However, as an identity issue - it is very important that we know to whom we belong and for what reason. Even though we aren't ever worthy of membership in God's family, it is still given to us. Once we were not a people, now we are God's people.

❖   ❖   ❖

Holy God, we long to belong to one another and to you so that we may know mercy and joy. Amen.

MAY ◆ 19

John 14:6
Jesus said to him, "I am the way, and the truth, and the life. No one comes to the Father except through me.

❖   ❖   ❖

We are a culture that not only wants but demands choices. We never want to be limited to one option. In this atmosphere, this verse is not comforting but annoying. We want more ways and other truths. We don't want exclusivity. We want options even when it comes to God. We want. We want. We want. Interestingly, God is looking at us and saying, "What do they need? They need a savior." We do have the freedom to choose to ignore what we need and continue a life of wanting. We can quibble with God's methods, but in the end, we cannot create and implement a way of truth and life for the sake of the world. We may have only one option, but it is a very, very good option. Ours is not to condemn those who do not agree but love as we have been loved.

❖   ❖   ❖

Holy God, forgive us and lead us into the truth of your mercy. Amen.

MAY ◆ 20

Psalm 98
Sing to the Lord a new song, for he has done marvelous things.

❖   ❖   ❖

As unsympathetic children, I remember when we would listen to someone's complaint and then raise our hands rubbing our thumb and forefinger in tiny circles - "Two of the smallest turn-tables in the world playing "My Heart Bleeds for You" in stereo. (I am not sure how that could be translated today's electronic devices, but I digress.) I can't imagine the number of times the Lord might have felt like doing the same thing to us. His grace deserves a new song from us once in a while.

❖   ❖   ❖

O Lord, help us to sing the new song in our lives. Amen.

MAY ◆ 21

Acts 17:30-31
While God has overlooked the times of human ignorance, now he commands all people everywhere to repent, because he has fixed a day on which he will have the world judged in righteousness by a man whom he has appointed, and of this he has given assurance to all by raising him from the dead.

❖ ❖ ❖

Christ came first to the people of Israel and his disciples were those who had grown up hearing the history of patriarchs and prophets and kings. The next people to hear the good news about Jesus were the Gentiles who had no encounters with Hebrew stories. Paul was called to be the one who would travel hundreds of miles, endure persecution for the sake of translating the story into words and ideas that could be understood by everyone. Paul had been the quintessential Hebrew with little interest beyond his closed world. Encountering Jesus exploded the boundaries of his world. Such is the power of the testimony of a changed life. Jesus rocks our world.

❖ ❖ ❖

Holy God, expand our world so that there are no limits to the reaches of your Good News. Amen.

MAY ◆ 22

Job 38:1-4

Then the Lord answered Job out of the whirlwind: "Who is this that darkens counsel by words without knowledge? Gird up your loins like a man, I will question you, and you shall declare to me. "Where were you when I laid the foundation of the earth? Tell me, if you have understanding.

❖ ❖ ❖

The "God is Dead" declarations of the 60's evolved from the trend of thought that God was really a mental invention of human beings. The idea of God helped to explain the unexplainable as they view the world. As our science developed we became more sophisticated in our understanding of ourselves and the world. Our need for an explanation of the mysterious evaporated. For some that meant the idea of God had lived out its purpose. Humans were more grown up now. The idea of God could die because we didn't need such an idea anymore. We could rest on our own abilities and put aside a notion of a being greater than ourselves. Humans of every age are free to embrace that assumption. I tried it once for a few days. After a while, it felt lonely, more like a lie and far more closed-minded. We haven't outgrown our need for God. We just have our days when we are a little too full of ourselves. God has a right to ask us to step outside for a little chat.

❖ ❖ ❖

Holy God, forgive us when we forget who we are and fail to enjoy your blessed company. Amen.

MAY ◆ 23

John 14:19-21
In a little while the world will no longer see me, but you will see me; because I live, you also will live. On that day you will know that I am in my Father, and you in me, and I in you. They who have my commandments and keep them are those who love me; and those who love me will be loved by my Father, and I will love them and reveal myself to them."

❖ ❖ ❖

I went to bed last night thinking of the points I forgot to make with the confirmation class the night before. We have their attention for such a small amount of time and they give us their attention an even smaller amount of time. But in that nanosecond of teaching opportunity we are allowed into the caverns of their growing souls, I want them to have the best of everything I can offer about the God who loves and forgives them and calls them to a life of compassion. The challenge, as teachers and parents, is being at our best the moment when those windows of opportunity happen. We can only try and hope. Our God, however, is always at the ready to reveal himself to us to make his love known.

❖ ❖ ❖

Holy God, reveal your love to us every day so that we can live our lives out loud for you. Amen.

MAY ◆ 24

Acts 1:6-8
So when they had come together, they asked him, "Lord, is this the time when you will restore the kingdom to Israel?" He replied, "It is not for you to know the times or periods that the Father has set by his own authority. But you will receive power when the Holy Spirit has come upon you; and you will be my witnesses in Jerusalem, in all Judea and Samaria, and to the ends of the earth."

❖ ❖ ❖

It never ceases to amaze me that the Gospel message spread so powerfully throughout the world without the internet, television news, radio or the telegraph or printing press. From one person to the next God's word of love and grace radiated out from a city in the Middle East to neighboring regions to places on earth no one at the time imagined existing. Restoring the kingdom to Israel was a small matter compared to the vision of a world embraced by God's love. We are still a part of that far flung activity of God's spirit reaching out to others.

❖ ❖ ❖

Holy God, help us to realize the power within us to share your blessed word. Amen.

MAY ◆ 25

Psalm 68-1-3
Let God rise up, let his enemies be scattered; let those who hate him flee before him. As smoke is driven away, so drive them away; as wax melts before the fire, let the wicked perish before God. But let the righteous be joyful; let them exult before God; let them be jubilant with joy.

❖ ❖ ❖

When I got a puppy I rediscovered the wonder of having something relentlessly joyful to see me. I am her human that gives her food, shelter, affection, toys, health care and a safe yard to do her business. She wants for nothing. She has the freedom to be utterly herself which happily includes being a little goofy when I appear. How could God want anything less for us than the freedom to be completely ourselves, at peace inside our own skin and thrilled beyond reason to be in his presence?

❖ ❖ ❖

Holy God, help us to be ever mindful of your care, provision and presence in our lives. Amen.

MAY ◆ 26

I Peter 5:
In the same way, you who are younger must accept the authority of the elders. And all of you must clothe yourselves with humility in your dealings with one another, for "God opposes the proud, but gives grace to the humble." Humble yourselves therefore under the mighty hand of God, so that he may exalt you in due time. Cast all your anxiety on him, because he cares for you.

❖   ❖   ❖

The young must accept authority of the elders, but we all must be humble in our dealings with one another. As hard as it is for the young to be respectful, it is just as hard for the older ones to be humble. There has to be good order in our lives together. At the same time, we need to reverence the life of each person in our presence. Whether or not they are members of our family, strangers or friends, in need or having something to offer, we are to recognize the royalty of all as children of God. Sometimes that is as simple as remembering to listen.

❖   ❖   ❖

Holy God, we listen to your word and ask for the strength to honor it with our own. Amen.

MAY ◆ 27

Psalm 150:6
Let everything that breathes praise the Lord! Praise the Lord!

❖   ❖   ❖

One the Discovery Channel, I learned about a strange looking fish called a mudskipper that crawls up on muddy flats out of the water, sucks mud to eat, leaps into the air to attract a mate, digs holes in the mud with its mouth and spits mud out to build a space for eggs. And if THAT wasn't amazing enough, the space where the eggs are laid are surrounded by mud and water-filled canals. The fish eggs will run out of air before they can hatch and so the mudskipper daddy gobbles air, swims up through the water and breathes into the egg chamber. Over and over and over again. The mudskipper doesn't have much time in the day to praise the Lord. I will do it for him. Will you join me?

❖   ❖   ❖

You, Lord, are amazing! Amen.

MAY ◆ 28

2 Samuel 1:26
I am distressed for you, my brother Jonathan; greatly beloved were you to me.

❖   ❖   ❖

At Texas A&M University, there is a much-loved tradition called Muster. In the spring of every year, the students gather for one evening and solemnly read the names of any current or former student who has died that year. As they call the roll, friends and family, light a candle and say, "Here!" as a way of claiming that their loved one is not forgotten and continues to be present if only in their memories. David mourned the loss in battle of his friend Jonathan and his grief was so profound that even to this day we do not remember Jonathan so much as a prince of Israel or a mighty warrior. We remember him mostly as a greatly loved friend. Tombstones often have very little room for exploits, accomplishments, awards or accolades. The few precious words are saved for relationships. Words like Beloved. God made sure that "beloved" is never far away from our name.

❖   ❖   ❖

God be with those we have lost and let us see our loved ones again. Amen.

MAY ♦ 29

John 6:15
He withdrew again to the mountain by himself.

❖   ❖   ❖

I like to go fishing. When you are fishing, people leave you alone without too much conversation. Parents even hush their children sometimes because "It will scare the fish." I can stare at my line and let the concerns of the world sit at a distance. One summer, I was fishing at a lake that was safely distant from forest fires that were burning in another area. But the wind shifted and the plumes of smoke blocked the sun. Low-flying planes and helicopters used to fight the flames pounded the air with war-like noises. In his time to be alone away from crowds, Jesus must have felt the gathering firestorm. People wanted him as their king because he provided them with food or could heal their illnesses. Others hated him for the threat he posed to their position of authority. Few understood the scope of the purpose of why he had really come. He came down the mountain and let the world invade his privacy.

❖   ❖   ❖

Lord, in our quiet time alone teach us how to face the firestorms of our lives. Amen.

MAY ◆ 30

John 8:58-59
"I tell you, before Abraham was, I am." So they picked up stones to throw at him.

❖   ❖   ❖

My father died when I was a teenager. He was my hero. My white knight. His death meant that as I began to grow into my adulthood my concept of him did not grow with me. He was forever crystallized in my memory in the heroic proportions of my teenage years. Years later stories of his life and encounters with people began to filter into my consciousness. It was then that I realized my father was just a guy, a regular guy with strengths and weaknesses as anyone else. For hundreds of years, Abraham was the icon of leadership and faithfulness. He was the first great human link to God. With Jesus a new link to God had come in far greater proportions that even Abraham could have imagined. It hurts to lose our heroes or have them dethroned but that is the truth of human life. Far more tragic is to not to see the heroism that is Jesus in our midst.

❖   ❖   ❖

Lord God, we thank you for being the champion of grace and truth in our world and in our lives. Amen.

MAY ◆ 31

John 8:43
Why do you not understand what I say? It is because you cannot accept my word.

❖ ❖ ❖

Ministering to friends and family sometimes is as simple and as difficult as listening well and asking good questions. Conversation is fundamentally important to the fabric of our lives and relationships and yet we often forget the basics. To give another person the gift of our attention and our effort to understand is not to be underestimated in its importance. To listen without filling our heads with our judgment or next response requires almost a physical effort on our part. When we disagree with what the person is saying or dislike the person, the effort to listen and understand is severely diminished. Of those who surrounded Christ there were those who listened and those who only sought to win an argument against him. The ones who learned to listen were changed forever.

❖ ❖ ❖

Lord, may we lay aside our need to win so that we may allow you to win the victory for us. Amen.

JUNE ◆ 1

Mark 9:43
If your hand causes you to stumble, cut it off

❖   ❖   ❖

Mark uses words in his Gospel like a scalpel. Sharp. To the point. Effective. The language he uses is sometimes "over the top" but his message is clear. Our relationship to God makes everything expendable. We are rarely placed in a position where we would have to choose God over all else. We do, however, have a tendency to keep all our options open rather than make choices. When we need to eliminate that which is hurting the most important relationships and we don't make the tough decisions, our lives quickly become cluttered and unmanageable. Mark's tough words are a warning. Stumbling blocks come in all shapes and forms: Addictions, indifference, toxic relationships. We tend to cling to the clutter instead of dealing with it. The problem, however, is not the clutter but what the clutter prevents us from seeing. This Gospel statement is a bold and radical proclamation that nothing is more important than who we are to God.

❖   ❖   ❖

God, keep us free from the clutter which chokes our ability to enjoy our life in you. Amen.

JUNE ♦ 2

John 5: 8
Jesus said to him, "Stand up, take your mat and walk."

❖   ❖   ❖

When working for a crisis information center, I took phone calls that often started with a long story. My job was to listen, to identify the problem and to refer the person to the best services to help. Sometimes the problem was simple to identify and sometimes we just had to ask the person "what do you really need right now?" The next step was to give them something to do. Often being in crisis is a feeling that we are stuck, immobilized without options. To do something, even the smallest of steps, helps us regain a sense of power in our lives. Jesus heals a man who is unable to walk and gives him something to do. The power of the gift Jesus gives us is when we use it. Works the same with love.

❖   ❖   ❖

Holy God, may we know the power of a life blessed to be a blessing to others. Amen.

JUNE ◆ 3

John 5: 33-35
'If I testify about myself, my testimony is not true. There is another who testifies on my behalf, and I know that his testimony to me is true. You sent messengers to John, and he testified to the truth. Not that I accept such human testimony, but I say these things so that you may be saved. He was a burning and shining lamp, and you were willing to rejoice for a while in his light. He was a burning and shining lamp

❖   ❖   ❖

In my office there is a framed calligraphy of a Japanese kanji character for the word "passion." Whenever my energy wanes it helps to remind me of the passion which the Gospel evokes. John the Baptist blew the dust off the promise of God to send a Savior to the people. He was a wild character who wore strange clothes and ate different food and bellowed for repentance. When the crowds gathered to hear and respond to his passionate message, he pointed away from himself to the one who was coming. He was both prophet and disciple. I like to be reminded of passion like John's. The good news of Christ is not just a warm fuzzy, but a passionate flame.

❖   ❖   ❖

Lord God, Burn your Gospel light in us so that others may know Christ's love. Amen.

JUNE ◆ 4

John 7:34
You will search for me, but you will not find me; and where I am, you cannot come.

❖ ❖ ❖

"When do you think you will miss your grandma the most?" I asked the dead woman's little granddaughter. I was trying to engage the forlorn-looking child engulfed in a sea of sad adult faces in the funeral home. "Right now" she said. My heart was wrenched by the clarity of her answer. This little one was dealing with the turbulent wake of death in which we seek out the loved one but can't find them. At such frightening moments in the past, her grandmother would have been there to quiet her fears, enfold her in soft arms and create laughter that would rumble through the top of her head. But death separates us from part of ourselves and leaves us in pieces. Jesus went to face and defeat that death so that right now we have who we need to face all that life and death throw at us.

❖ ❖ ❖

Lord God, when we walk through the valley of death help us to know that you are right here. Amen.

JUNE ◆ 5

John 7:37
"Let anyone who is thirsty come to me."

❖   ❖   ❖

Someone once said that one of the weaknesses of Christianity is Christians. The tactics that some Christians use to invite or rather coerce people into a life of faith are embarrassing. On a college campus, an itinerant preacher frequently parks himself outside the student center where he can rant at the passing students. He criticizes their clothes, their attitudes. He barks at them with judgment and tries to frighten them with visions of hell in their future. He bears the name of Christ like a permit to be offensive. We were not sent to offend people into the kingdom but to offer to those who are hungry and thirsty a way to find peace inside their own skin. The cross of Christ where a sinless man died for the sins of the world is offensive enough.

❖   ❖   ❖

Holy God, give us the courage to witness to what we have known and to do it with compassion. Amen.

JUNE ◆ 6

Isaiah 66:12
For thus says the Lord: I will extend prosperity to her like a river, and the wealth of the nations like an overflowing stream

❖ ❖ ❖

I went on a "little" canoe trip with some youth and adults from our church after they worked on two Habitat projects. My arms and knees do not consider anything that is measured in miles as "little" and this was a 6-mile trip. Our canoe flipped once and we got an unplanned splash in the muddy waters of the river. My camera got ruined. My arms felt like sacks of wet sand. More than once, I questioned my own sanity. At the same time, I knew that God had extended wealth to me, not only like a river, but on a river. There was wealth in the constant laughter even as we were tired and thought the trip would never end. There was wealth in knowing that my canoe mate and I would have a memory that would make us laugh every time we told it. There was wealth in the journey with those who choose to work and play with one another in God's name.

❖ ❖ ❖

Praise God from whom all blessings flow. Amen.

JUNE ◆ 7

Mark 8:34
If any want to become my followers, let them deny themselves and take up their cross.

❖ ❖ ❖

Being a follower is not usually a compliment. It is sometimes used in reference to youth who are vulnerable to falling into risky behaviors. We don't want our children to be followers without being discriminating. The fact is that we do follow all the time. We will adopt the accent of our family. We mimic without thinking the habits of our parents. We are persuaded by the advertisers who convince us that we need what they have to offer. That we will follow is a given. Who we follow is still our choice. Jesus never forced anyone. He never justified the means with the end. He was quite clear to his disciples that his way was the cross. Jesus gained followers by telling us the truth.

❖ ❖ ❖

Lord God, give us the courage to face the truth and to follow in your way. Amen.

JUNE ◆ 8

Psalm 5:8
Lead me, O Lord, in your righteousness because of my enemies; make your way straight before me.

❖   ❖   ❖

I was on my way to a conference in a strange city. My flight delayed me by several hours and it was well after midnight by the time the cab drove to the darkened conference center surrounded by a large fence. The cab driver walked around the building with me and we found a rock propping open a gate. Through the gate, we found one lighted room and there we found my name on a piece of paper next to a room key. We found the room and the cab driver didn't leave until I was safely locked inside. We tend to make our own path in the world until we don't recognize landmarks anymore and we lose the light. In those dark, lost moments we are most willing to be led for good and for ill. A rock, a lighted room, a piece of paper, a key, a patient cab driver were the urban bread crumbs that God set before me one night to make straight my path. It never ceases to amaze me that no matter which path we take, God will have been there ahead of us.

❖   ❖   ❖

Lord God, may we be quick to see the evidence of your righteousness spread out before us. Amen.

JUNE ◆ 9

Mark 9:19
How much longer must I put up with you? Bring him to me."

❖ ❖ ❖

Most school children figure out quickly that when a teacher asks the class a question, the teacher will answer it eventually. They sweat out the moment of being called upon, but it will pass and the truth will be revealed. The disciples of Jesus were still school children learning their way in a brave, new vision of the kingdom. They tried to heal a boy, but could not. Jesus expresses the frustration of a teacher wondering when the students will finally get it. Then Jesus says, "Bring him to me." Even from the depths of his own disappointment, Jesus offers grace to the boy and his disciples. God is certainly free to be disappointed and frustrated with us as reluctant students of his will. But students who know their teacher endure the discomfort of the moment in order to hear the word of grace and hope. When what we are attempting fails miserably, we can hear God say, "Bring it to me."

❖ ❖ ❖

Holy God, forgive us when we fall short of understanding your will and your ways. Amen.

JUNE ◆ 10

Matthew 6:33-34
But strive first for the kingdom of God and his righteousness, and all these things will be given to you as well. "So do not worry about tomorrow, for tomorrow will bring worries of its own. Today's trouble is enough for today.

❖   ❖   ❖

Don't worry. Yeah, right. The bills still need to be paid. Children need daily attention. Gas prices are out of control. Joints ache and allergies abound. Pressure at work to produce is relentless. We don't have to look for things to worry about - they sit on our heads and twist our backs and rake our internal organs. We don't want a God who just sits next to us and pats us on the hand and assures us that we are not alone. We want action. We don't want or need a God who is unable or unwilling to do something on our behalf. So God sent his Son, we acted and he died. God acted and he rose again from the dead. Now let's listen to ourselves again as we tell him what we are worried about.

❖   ❖   ❖

By the cross of your Son, Lord, we are freed from the worry that robs us of our lives. Amen.

JUNE ◆ 11

Psalm 104:25- 26
Yonder is the sea, great and wide, creeping things innumerable are there, living things both small and great. There go the ships, and Leviathan that you formed to sport in it.

❖   ❖   ❖

During a trip to Hawaii, I had the privilege of drinking my morning coffee watching whales. They were swimming with their young calves in the warm waters before making the long journey up north. They jumped. They swam in circles. They slapped their tails on the surface of the water. I have been intrigued recently with the story of some wayward whales swimming in the Sacramento River. Every effort was being made to herd them back to the open ocean but they seemed content to do what they wanted to do. As much as we know, we continue to discover how much we don't know about the mysteries of God's creation. Sometimes the best thing we can do is simply be in awe.

❖   ❖   ❖

Master Designer, may we wander with reverence and awe through the masterpiece of your world. Amen.

JUNE ◆ 12

Romans 8:22-25
We know that the whole creation has been groaning in labor pains until now; and not only the creation, but we ourselves, who have the first fruits of the Spirit, groan inwardly while we wait for adoption, the redemption of our bodies. For in hope we were saved. Now hope that is seen is not hope. For who hopes for what is seen? But if we hope for what we do not see, we wait for it with patience.

❖ ❖ ❖

I have a friend who is anticipating the birth of a child in less than a few weeks. The pregnancy, though relatively normal, has still been fraught with all the anxieties that living sometimes brings. Health, work, financial concerns. worry for the serious illness of extended family. The process of getting the first child to make room in her mind and heart and world of toys for a little sister. And even though ultrasound pictures reveal a little body and a recognizable face, there is still the waiting for that moment when she arrives and she is given a name and she becomes her own person in this family. We are little ones still waiting to come into the fullness of God's kingdom. God has been fretting and preparing for us.

❖ ❖ ❖

Holy God, knowing that you are laboring over us, we wait with patience and work with hope. Amen.

JUNE ◆ 13

John 14:23
Jesus answered him, "Those who love me will keep my word, and my Father will love them, and we will come to them and make our home with them.

❖   ❖   ❖

In the movie "Finding Nemo," Dora, the memory-challenged fish says to her friend Marlin, "Please don't go away. Please? No one's ever stuck with me for so long before. And if you leave... if you leave... I just, I remember things better with you...... I remember it, I do. It's there, I know it is, because when I look at you, I can feel it. And-and I look at you, and I... and I'm home." There are people in my life and, I hope in yours, who when we look at them - we are home. When the people of God take to heart the power of the Gospel and love as they have been loved, then no one will ever be homeless. The Christian faith is not just a private relationship in which we individually find our home in Christ. It is most completely what God intended when we love God and one another.

❖   ❖   ❖

Lord God, may another look at us today and see your home for them in us. Amen.

JUNE ◆ 14

Galatians 6:7-10
Do not be deceived; God is not mocked, for you reap whatever you sow. If you sow to your own flesh, you will reap corruption from the flesh; but if you sow to the Spirit, you will reap eternal life from the Spirit. So let us not grow weary in doing what is right, for we will reap at harvest time, if we do not give up. So then, whenever we have an opportunity, let us work for the good of all, and especially for those of the family of faith.

❖   ❖   ❖

When injustice seems to win more often than justice...When crime seems to pay.... When one whose gifts are no better than yours seems to be enjoying blessing upon blessing.....it is easy to weary of doing what is right. And so we reach for some motivation. Looking to what we have been given without comparing ourselves to others, the thanksgiving still overflows. With the thanks comes the simple motivation of a grateful heart. Led by the spirit of gratitude we are led step by step to stranger and friend to work for good.

❖   ❖   ❖

Lord, help us not to weary of being your faithful people. Amen.

JUNE ◆ 15

Proverbs 8:1-3, 10-11
Does not wisdom call, and does not understanding raise her voice? On the heights, beside the way, at the crossroads she takes her stand; beside the gates in front of the town, at the entrance of the portals she cries out: Take my instruction instead of silver, and knowledge rather than choice gold; for wisdom is better than jewels, and all that you may desire cannot compare with her.

❖ ❖ ❖

Wisdom, according to the author of Proverbs, is readily accessible. Wisdom is out there. Wisdom is available at the mall and the main streets. Why is it that when we are faced with difficulties, we feel so cut off from the source of any good advice? Friends might tell what they would do but don't offer any other options. Sometimes friends are reluctant to give us advice, to tell us what they really think and believe. They want to honor our freedom to make our own decisions to the point of leaving us in a vacuum to fend for ourselves. God gives us all the wisdom that we need but neither does God design us to be self-sufficient to the point of needing no one. We are designed to be a people working together. We have within us wisdom to share and the need for wisdom outside ourselves. With compassion, it is possible to leave arrogance at home so that we can recognize wisdom when we hear it in one another and offer it with love and humility.

❖ ❖ ❖

Holy God, make us wise enough to know what we know and what we don't know. Amen.

JUNE ◆ 16

John 17:1-4
After Jesus had spoken these words, he looked up to heaven and said, Father, the hour has come; glorify your Son so that the Son may glorify you, since you have given him authority over all people, to give eternal life to all whom you have given him. And this is eternal life, that they may know you, the only true God, and Jesus Christ whom you have sent. I glorified you on earth by finishing the work that you gave me to do.

❖ ❖ ❖

Jesus brought honor to God by finishing the work assigned to him. When we were given report cards in school, a notation of "incomplete" was often a last ditch extension of grace on the part of the teacher to finish the work and prevent the inevitable failing grade. Sometimes I wonder if God has not given the whole world a grade of "incomplete" so that we might take this time of grace to finish the work he gave us to do. I've witnessed many people who have given up. Given up parenting, given up loving, given up civility, given up compassion, given up generosity. Giving up is always an option. It is an option Jesus had the freedom to choose. Instead, he finished the work God gave him to do which was granting us an extension so that we could finish too.

❖ ❖ ❖

Help us, O God, never to take for granted the work you have given us to do and the grace you have given us with which to do it. Amen.

JUNE ◆ 17

Mark 4:40
He said to them, "Why are you afraid? Have you still no faith?" And they were filled with great awe and said to one another, "Who then is this, that even the wind and the sea obey him?"

❖ ❖ ❖

When I am afraid, the "fight or flight" response is kicked into high gear. Do I defend myself? Wrestle with the problem or the person? Or do I look for the exit signs? When I am in awe, I have a tendency to stand still. I stare. I look. I look again. The rest of the world falls away and I find a little oasis of peace in an often turbulent day. On that day in a boat at sea with his disciples, Jesus turned fear into awe. When we are afraid of God and the truth about ourselves, we either argue about God or we avoid an opportunity to encounter God all together. Growth in faith happens when we move from "fight or flight" in our relationship with God to standing at peace in His presence.

❖ ❖ ❖

Holy God, still our noisy storms and help us find our peace in you. Amen.

JUNE ◆ 18

Acts 2:17-18
'In the last days it will be, God declares, that I will pour out my Spirit upon all flesh, and your sons and your daughters shall prophesy, and your young men shall see visions, and your old men shall dream dreams. Even upon my slaves, both men and women, in those days I will pour out my Spirit; and they shall prophesy.

❖ ❖ ❖

The Spirit of God is no respecter of age, economic estate, or gender. The idea of God allowing such access to the power and truth of his spirit to a culture which defined itself by denying access was mind boggling. Pentecost was God's big bang theory of the universe. To a relatively small gathering of distinctly different people the Spirit was given. What might have been just an interesting chapter in the history of humanity became a wildfire that spread throughout the world and through generations. I know enough about human beings to know that we are just not that good and effective to make such amazing things come to pass. One of the great witnesses to the truth of the Gospel of Jesus Christ is the Church itself that became a dynamic force moving outward at Pentecost.

❖ ❖ ❖

Lord God, we have within us the ability to recognize the truth when we hear it. We rejoice in the sound. Amen.

June ◆ 19

Psalm 104:31-32
May the glory of the Lord endure forever; may the Lord rejoice in his works-who looks on the earth and it trembles, who touches the mountains and they smoke.

❖   ❖   ❖

One of the ways in which we show that we are truly made in the image of God is when we create something. The creation may be a work of art or a project or a solution to a problem. There is often that moment when we step back, realizing the work is finished, and we rejoice. We rejoice that it is finished and we rejoice in admiration of the wonder of it. It is this powerful moment of knowing the Creator God whose spirit courses through our veins. God gives us the opportunity to create and enjoy the work of our own hand or the product of our own imagination. It just gets mind-boggling when we think of God looking at us and dancing.

❖   ❖   ❖

Blessed are you, O Lord, maker of heaven and earth. Amen.

JUNE ◆ 20

I Kings 19:19,21b
So he set out from there, and found Elisha son of Shaphat, who was plowing. There were twelve yoke of oxen ahead of him, and he was with the twelfth. Elijah passed by him and threw his mantle over him. Then he set out and followed Elijah, and became his servant.

❖   ❖   ❖

The mantle was a piece of clothing - a sleeveless garment - symbolizing leadership and authority. The more modern version is the stole which ordained clergy wear as a symbol of leadership and the yoke of the pastoral office. Hard to tell what was going through Elisha's mind when he was picked, but he had to be, at least, a little naive if he thought the work of a prophet was easier than standing behind a plow. The work to which we have all been called is one which we would slough off when the going got tough were it not for God who has called us to this task. The mantle of leadership can be heavy, cumbersome, and uncomfortable but the one who put it on us loves us, believes in us, and gives us what we need for the day ahead. Sometimes just one day at a time.

❖   ❖   ❖

Holy God, grant us the grace to accept the work to which you have called us. Amen.

JUNE ◆ 21

Matthew 6:19-21
"Do not store up for yourselves treasures on earth, where moth and rust consume and where thieves break in and steal; but store up for yourselves treasures in heaven, where neither moth nor rust consumes and where thieves do not break in and steal. For where your treasure is, there your heart will be also.

❖ ❖ ❖

I drove a 1969 Datsun 510 when I was on internship. The floor boards rusted out from wheel well to wheel well. The junk dealer gave me an extra $25. - just for having the courage to drive it to the junkyard. It left large chunks of itself in my parking space at church. A member picked up a chunk one day and painted this verse on it and gave it to me as a present. It is a constant reminder that things fall apart. That car had been my first experience with driving a stick shift. It got me where I needed to go. But it couldn't carry me all the way. In our journey of faith, many come and go. Many dreams come and go. We are dust and to dust we shall return. When the dust settles and the rust is swept away, there is Jesus ready to carry us the rest of the way.

❖ ❖ ❖

Remember us, Lord, when you come into your kingdom. Amen.

JUNE ◆ 22

2 Corinthians 4:1
Therefore, since it is by God's mercy that we are engaged in this ministry, we do not lose heart.

❖   ❖   ❖

I misplace things. That sounds so much better than "lose." If I don't put my keys on the kitchen counter every day, I have to look for them because I put them somewhere that I don't usually put them. They are not lost. I have misplaced them. I have always been able to find them again; though, the older I get, the more that possibility of not finding them rears its head. So with that in mind, I have to admit that I have not lost heart but I have misplaced it on several occasions. The feelings are similar to losing heart. It feels hollow and heavy, but the moment vanishes swiftly when I crawl into God's presence and find him securely holding my wandering heart. So when at times we experience hollow days and heaviness of purpose, we may not even be able to articulate what is wrong. But if we crawl again into God's waiting arms, we find our heart again even before we know that we had ever lost it.

❖   ❖   ❖

God of mercy, may we always find ourselves in you. Amen.

JUNE ♦ 23

Luke 21:10-13
Then he said to them, "Nation will rise against nation, and kingdom against kingdom; there will be great earthquakes, and in various places famines and plagues; and there will be dreadful portents and great signs from heaven. "But before all this occurs, they will arrest you and persecute you; they will hand you over to synagogues and prisons, and you will be brought before kings and governors because of my name. This will give you an opportunity to testify.

❖ ❖ ❖

This is one of those "Aside from that, Mrs. Lincoln, how did you like the play?" kind of verses. The opportunity to witness to faith in the midst of horrific turmoil and threat of death probably wasn't received with great joy. We, who have the perspective of history, know that those first generation Christians did, in fact, testify courageously to the Good News of Jesus Christ. In the face of tremendous hardship, they refused to submit to the tyrannical leaders that would silence them. Their witness fueled the spread of the faith throughout the world and into new generations. The social acceptability of Christianity has dampened the fervor for witness. We still have battles to fight. We still have earthquakes of injustice and hunger. There is no more important time for us to be the living witness to Christ in our midst. The arena is filled with all the saints who have gone before us cheering us on.

❖ ❖ ❖

Holy God, we ride on the shoulders of our brothers and sisters who were the first champions of the faith. For their witness, we give you thanks. Amen.

JUNE ◆ 24

Genesis 1:1-2
In the beginning when God created the heavens and the earth, the earth was a formless void and darkness covered the face of the deep, while a wind from God swept over the face of the waters.

❖   ❖   ❖

I think it is interesting when scientists are exploring the universe looking for intelligent life that one of the signs they seek on the surface of a planet is an orderly pattern. Besides the random patterns made by mountain ranges and ancient riverbeds and meteor craters, they look for an order out of the void that indicates some purpose, some plan. The streets that create a fabric of lines, the highways and patchwork crop patterns are order out of chaos. We establish boundaries so that we can control our world within its confines. We do that every day in tiny ways within our jobs and our households. In that way we both reflect the image of the Creator and dangle our toes dangerously on the edge of trying to be God within our little realms. We do well to remember how small we are and how big God is.

❖   ❖   ❖

Help us, Lord, to remember the vastness of your creative hand. Amen.

JUNE ◆ 25

Psalm 8:3-5
When I look at your heavens, the work of your fingers, the moon and the stars that you have established; what are human beings that you are mindful of them, mortals that you care for them? Yet you have made them a little lower than God, and crowned them with glory and honor.

❖   ❖   ❖

There is a moment in the evenings when I am in transit from car to door or door to car when I look at the night sky. I will notice how low the clouds are hanging or how swiftly they are moving in the gulf winds. I will notice a star or the lights of a passing plane that moves silently in the dark. I will notice the sliver of a moon or the varied shadows of its craters. In that tiny moment, I know of a peace that betrays the events of the day and a sense of endless wonder that God has chosen to paint me into this majestic canvas.

❖   ❖   ❖

Well done, Lord, well done. Amen.

JUNE ◆ 26

2 Corinthians 13:5-14
Examine yourselves to see whether you are living in the faith. Test yourselves. Do you not realize that Jesus Christ is in you? -unless, indeed, you fail to meet the test! I hope you will find out that we have not failed.

❖ ❖ ❖

It has been the plot of movies - a person wakes up from having been in a coma for years only to discover that their former life and relationships are a thing of the past. Sin is like a drug-induced coma. We forget who we are and whose we are and float aimlessly in a sea of hazy ideas in which we feel disconnected from everything and everyone. To be alive in the faith is not something we do but something we are. When we know who and whose we are then we move not in a groggy stupor but in a clarity which understands our purpose.

❖ ❖ ❖

Lord God, we believe that Christ is alive in us. Amen.

JUNE ◆ 27

Matthew 28:16-20
Now the eleven disciples went to Galilee, to the mountain to which Jesus had directed them. When they saw him, they worshiped him; but some doubted. And Jesus came and said to them, "All authority in heaven and on earth has been given to me. Go therefore and make disciples of all nations, baptizing them in the name of the Father and of the Son and of the Holy Spirit, and teaching them to obey everything that I have commanded you. And remember, I am with you always, to the end of the age."

❖ ❖ ❖

Even as they doubted, Jesus gave them authority and a charge to make disciples. The testimony to the power of the spirit and the integrity of God's promise is in this fact: thousands of years and miles removed from when those words were first spoken to those eleven guys, you are reading it again so that your discipleship might grow. It is an overwhelming responsibility we have been given but we have been given the authority to do it. I read recently that the only time we waste is the time we spend thinking we are alone. Christ is with us always.

❖ ❖ ❖

Holy God, you grant us the privilege of your company for purposes beyond personal comfort. You have sent us for a purpose. Amen.

JUNE ◆ 28

Psalm 29
The voice of the Lord splits the flames of fire; the voice of the Lord shakes the wilderness; the Lord shakes the wilderness of Kadesh. The voice of the Lord makes the oak tree writhe and strips the forest bare.....the Lord shall give strength to his people; the Lord shall give his people the blessing of peace.

❖ ❖ ❖

The song of the psalmist is one which almost brags about how big and tough the Lord is. If God wanted to be a bully, no one could argue with him. God has the strength to squash, obliterate, decimate, terrify, and destroy. God chooses to protect, guide, strengthen, and honor the dignity of his own fragile and flawed creation. God gives us the same choice in our relationships with one another.

❖ ❖ ❖

Give us, O Lord, a gentle hand and a patient ear. Amen.

JUNE ◆ 29

I Corinthians 4:5
Therefore do not pronounce judgment before the time, before the Lord comes, who will bring to light the things now hidden in darkness and will disclose the purposes of the heart. Then each one will receive commendation from God.

❖ ❖ ❖

It was the old Charlie Brown saying, "I love mankind. It's people I can't stand." We are naturally a judgmental lot. Well, I would like to think so because I don't want to be alone in the fact that I seem to lean toward the critical, especially when I am tired. We seem to be like construction workers sitting by a fence during a break watching people walk by and rating them according to some criteria that we have in our heads. If I have learned anything, it is that we never have the whole picture. We never see what can't be seen because we hide so well from one another. What is not hidden becomes the target for the judgment of others. God sees everything there is to see about us. We would be naive to think that he chooses to look the other way. He sent his son to the cross so that with grace and forgiveness, we would be pleasing in his sight, inside and out.

❖ ❖ ❖

Lord God, as we look to others help us to remember the grace with which you look at us. Amen.

JUNE ◆ 30

Jeremiah 23:3
Then I myself will gather the remnant of my flock out of all the lands where I have driven them, and I will bring them back to their fold, and they shall be fruitful and multiply.

❖ ❖ ❖

A remnant in a fabric store is a short amount of cloth at the end of a bolt usually not enough to make anything substantial. It may only be of value to those who only need a small piece, like a quilter. A remnant in the history of the people of God are those people who have stayed close to the core of their faith, their relationship with God. By themselves they were still unable to mount an army against an enemy or rise up a great nation, but God was always able to do amazing things with a remnant. The patchwork quilt of God's people is messy on one side and powerfully patterned on the other so that all may see the vision of God's handiwork. There are days when we may feel like a piece clinging to the end of the bolt questioning our value, but God blessed our history so that those days would pale in comparison to the days we can stand in awe and wonder at the Master Designer's ability to piece together scattered pieces with gracious threads.

❖ ❖ ❖

Creator of the Universe, take the remnant of our days and make them a witness to your grace and love. Amen.

JULY ◆ 1

Psalm 68:7-10
O God, when you went out before your people, when you marched through the wilderness, the earth quaked, the heavens poured down rain at the presence of God, the God of Sinai, at the presence of God, the God of Israel. Rain in abundance, O God, you showered abroad; you restored your heritage when it languished; your flock found a dwelling in it; in your goodness, O God, you provided for the needy.

❖ ❖ ❖

Our journey of faith is not a simple, even path meandering through a sweet meadow. It can be a slippery slope where two steps forward are truly met with more backward. Such it is in my own faith life. When faced with unexpected obstacles, I rear back - I lose my footing and balance and I grope for a handhold. The blessing of a life of faith is that we have a history of handholds to remember. God consistently has been there in the uncertainty. Handholds came to us in an assuring word, a burden shared, a prayer offered. Growth in our journey is measured not by the distance we have covered but by the times we become the handholds for others.

❖ ❖ ❖

Holy God, your Kingdom is coming. One by one, your Kingdom is coming. Amen.

JULY ♦ 2

John 2:5
His mother said to the servants, "Do whatever he tells you."

❖   ❖   ❖

Mary, the mother of Jesus, did not have to take her faith like a new car out for a test drive. She already knew that it worked. Mary was the first believer in Jesus. No one knew better in the early days of his ministry just who Jesus truly was. She could rest on her laurels as the first disciple. She had already served God well in bearing, laboring, and nurturing. Even still, she continued to follow and believe. At the wedding at Cana, she stepped out boldly in faith and was consequently rebuked for pushing God's timing. Mary did not shrink away or disagree with Jesus' rebuke as we might expect a mother to do. She did confidently instruct the servants to listen to Jesus. She knew that what he did from there was his business. Mary, as the first believer, does help to show us all how to walk with faith and humility and still point others to Jesus.

❖   ❖   ❖

Lord God, thank you for Mary and all of the believers who help us to walk in faith. Amen.

JULY ◆ 3

Psalm 34: 5-6
Look upon him and be radiant, and let not your faces be ashamed. I called in my affliction, and the Lord heard me and saved me from all my troubles. The angel of the Lord encompasses those who fear him and he will deliver them. Taste and see that the Lord is good; happy are they who trust in him.

❖   ❖   ❖

Sorrow and shame are things that when left uncheck will feed on themselves like a dog chasing its tail and stirring up dust on a hot summer day. The cycle must be broken. The furious spinning of empty, endless thoughts must find a new direction. In the presence of the Lord, it is hard not to look up and feel the cool kiss of a new day.

❖   ❖   ❖

Bless this day with your energy and hope, Lord. Amen.

JULY ◆ 4

Deuteronomy 11:18-21
You shall put these words of mine in your heart and soul, and you shall bind them as a sign on your hand, and fix them as an emblem on your forehead. Teach them to your children, talking about them when you are at home and when you are away, when you lie down and when you rise. Write them on the doorposts of your house and on your gates, so that your days and the days of your children may be multiplied in the land that the Lord swore to your ancestors to give them, as long as the heavens are above the earth.

❖ ❖ ❖

It is a thought done in hindsight. Why did I get so anxious? Why didn't I trust God? There is a sense of being hit upside the head with the words inside your own head "Why do you always have to make it so difficult?" As God was shaping the nation of Israel he called them to be vigilant to his word. He knew that their attention span was terrible even then. He called them to write it on their hands and post-it-note it to their doors. The words are "I am God. You are my people." We are to remember and say it over and again until it seeps into the pores of hard heads and into the pulsing highways of toughened hearts.

❖ ❖ ❖

You are God, Lord, and I am not. Help that wonderful fact to sink into me. Amen.

JULY ◆ 5

Psalm 31:9-14
Be gracious to me, O Lord, for I am in distress; my eye wastes away from grief, my soul and body also. For my life is spent with sorrow, and my years with sighing; my strength fails because of my misery, and my bones waste away. I am the scorn of all my adversaries, a horror to my neighbors, an object of dread to my acquaintances; those who see me in the street flee from me. I have passed out of mind like one who is dead; I have become like a broken vessel. For I hear the whispering of many- terror all around!- as they scheme together against me, as they plot to take my life. But I trust in you, O Lord; I say, "You are my God."

❖   ❖   ❖

The thing about sitcoms and television dramas is that there are always speedy problem resolutions. In less than an hour, the problem is shown and then the solution happens. Psalms occasionally sound like 30-second problem resolution. They start with stating the dilemma and in this case, life is downright awful. And then there is that insidious "But...." What comes after that "but" is usually a bold statement of faith for no apparent reason. Faith is not problem resolution. It is what carries us from being utterly stuck into the promise of a new blessing.

❖   ❖   ❖

Holy God, even out of the depths, we know that you hear us and call us to trust in you. Amen.

JULY ◆ 6

Ephesians 4:31-32
Put away from you all bitterness and wrath and anger and wrangling and slander, together will all malice, and be kind to one another, tenderhearted, forgiving one another, as God in Christ has forgiven you.

❖   ❖   ❖

If we ever wonder why reading the Bible daily is so important, this verse is a great example. It is a message we need to see over and over again. It is so easy to fall into the vortex of ugliness which blinds us to our own short comings and sharpens the rapier of our critique of others. Being kind and tenderhearted is no walk in the park though. To be kind to those who love us is easy. To be tenderhearted to those who have written us off as worthless is heroic and born of the cross. The word of God comes to us again and again in words to save our lives and anyone we meet.

❖   ❖   ❖

Holy God, cool our tempers and tender our words. Amen.

JULY ◆ 7

Ephesians 2:19-20
So then you are no longer strangers and aliens, but you are citizens with the saints and also members of the household of God, built upon the foundation of the apostles and prophets, with Christ Jesus himself as the cornerstone.

❖ ❖ ❖

"Give me your hand!" I heard a voice above and beyond me say with absolute surety and a growing hint of insistence. I was bouncing through the rapids of a fast-moving river in North Carolina having just been catapulted out of a raft. My glasses were dangling on the keeper cords around my neck but nowhere near my eyes. I couldn't see the float with the rope that the rescuers were trying to throw in my direction. The person throwing the float tossed again and again until the float hit me squarely on the head and I grabbed it. I was pulled to the side of a large boulder near the edge of the river and I heard the voice again, "Give me your hand." Instead of looking for the hand attached to the voice, I just reached out my hand. The hand of my rescuer found me. Sometimes I think the saints who have gone before us stand on the river's edge with hands and voices to lead us to solid ground.

❖ ❖ ❖

Holy God, grant us the will to live, the strength to believe in the face of the impossible, the faith to extend our hand. Amen.

JULY ◆ 8

I Kings 17:22-24
The Lord listened to the voice of Elijah; the life of the child came into him again, and he revived. Elijah took the child, brought him down from the upper chamber into the house, and gave him to his mother; then Elijah said, "See, your son is alive." So the woman said to Elijah, "Now I know that you are a man of God, and that the word of the Lord in your mouth is truth."

❖ ❖ ❖

The widow had been instructed by God to feed his prophet Elijah during a terrible time of drought and famine. She barely had enough food for herself and her son. God provided for them all. When the son fell severely ill, she was angry. Elijah prayed to God to restore the boy to health and God did. Then the woman believed that Elijah was a man of God. We continue to be a skeptical, stiff-necked, stubborn people when it comes to believing God with our whole heart, whole mind and, whole strength. We always hold something back. The kind of trust God wants to raise up in us is the whole enchilada.

❖ ❖ ❖

Lord God, help us to believe completely who you are and what you have promised. Amen.

JULY ◆ 9

Psalm 126:6
Those who go out weeping, bearing the seed for sowing, shall come home with shouts of joy, carrying their sheaves.

❖ ❖ ❖

It takes no small amount of courage to push out of sleep into the day full of the sorrows that keep one tossing all night. Out of utter fatigue, to wrestle to one's feet and shoulder the responsibilities of nurturing hope is the stuff of miracles. The courage and the energy comes from the only source of hope and joy and that has ever kept a promise - the God who gives us all that we need to battle weariness and champion the cause of love

❖ ❖ ❖

God of love, fill our hearts with hope and our minds with strength. Amen.

July ◆ 10

Galatians 1:21-24
Then I went into the regions of Syria and Cilicia, and I was still unknown by sight to the churches of Judea that are in Christ; they only heard it said, "The one who formerly was persecuting us is now proclaiming the faith he once tried to destroy." And they glorified God because of me.

❖ ❖ ❖

I was listening to a colleague recently talk about the challenges of evangelism. He said, "When in doubt, tell your story." In an age in which we think evangelism is done by those well-trained in debating and marketing techniques, it is no wonder we all shy away. The apostle Paul just told his story. Once he fought against Christians, now he was one of them. The power of the faith is revealed most especially in a changed life. The changes might not be as dramatic as Paul's were but the level of the change doesn't matter. God makes a difference in a life. God changes us from the inside out so that our story can give testimony to the God of grace and love.

❖ ❖ ❖

Holy God, give us the courage to tell our story so that others may know you. Amen.

July ◆ 11

Luke 7:15-17
The dead man sat up and began to speak, and Jesus gave him to his mother. Fear seized all of them; and they glorified God, saying, "A great prophet has risen among us!" and "God has looked favorably on his people!" This word about him spread throughout Judea and all the surrounding country.

❖   ❖   ❖

Scientists look for signs of life on other planets and we still look for signs of life on this one. As sophisticated as we have become in our understanding of how the world works, we are still hungry for signs that God is present and active. Life sometimes feels more like a series of problems than a blessed gift. Just because we have to be as vigilant as scientists in our looking for signs of divine life does not take away the wonder and amazement that God is, in fact, bombarding our days with a meteor shower of his grace.

❖   ❖   ❖

Help us, Lord, to look and see you alive in our world every day. Amen.

JULY ◆ 12

John 4:23
The true worshipers will worship the Father in spirit and truth.

❖ ❖ ❖

One of the great occupational hazards for pastors is that sometimes we forget to worship. Responsible for the mechanics of the worship celebration, we think more about what comes next than focusing on God. The danger of not paying attention to the task is stumbling or missing words. The last thing I want to do is have my mistake become the focus of attention, so there is some honor in getting it right. I have learned that it is not much different out in the pews where children are making faces or noises, someone is remembering the argument with a family member in the parking lot, or wondering what's for lunch. Even still, on the chords of a hymn, in the flicker of a candle, in the aroma of the bread, in the exquisite warmth of a human hand, in words almost too wonderful to understand completely, we worship together. Even still, the truth and the Spirit surround the people and in our feeble, distracted way we praise God.

❖ ❖ ❖

Lord God, receive the work of our worship as a gift to you who loves us so well. Amen.

JULY ◆ 13

2 Samuel 12:11-13
Thus says the Lord: I will raise up trouble against you from within your own house; and I will take your wives before your eyes, and give them to your neighbor, and he shall lie with your wives in the sight of this very sun. For you did it secretly; but I will do this thing before all Israel, and before the sun." David said to Nathan, "I have sinned against the Lord." Nathan said to David, "Now the Lord has put away your sin; you shall not die.

❖ ❖ ❖

It took Nathan verbally slapping David in the face with the magnitude of his sin and God's anger to get him to see what he had done. More often than not, when we sin, the collateral damage on other relationships is something we rarely take into consideration in the heat of the moment. David had used his power to kill and to satisfy a selfish desire. He damaged his relationship with God in the process. We all need Nathans who will courageously tell us the truth for the sake of keeping us inside the relationship that matters most.

❖ ❖ ❖

Holy God, help us to be quick to confess so that your forgiveness might restore us to righteousness. Amen.

JULY ◆ 14

John 6:8
One of his disciples, Andrew, Simon Peter's brother, said to him, "There is a boy here who has five barley loaves and two fish. But what are they among so many people?"

❖ ❖ ❖

The story has been repeated through human history countless times. The need is too great. The people in need are too many. What can any person really do? And the response of millions is "Nothing." What will a small gesture be in the midst of overwhelming need? The small effect becomes a foolish waste. Andrew sees a glimmer of possibility in a boy's armful of food, but his vision disintegrates into the realities of the statistics. Even still Jesus blesses the gesture. The story repeated gives us the opportunity again and again to choose between those standing empty handed in a desert of dry hope or moving with the faith that sees the Kingdom breaking into our world a handful at a time.

❖ ❖ ❖

Help us, Lord, to choose life by believing that all things are possible. Amen.

JULY ◆ 15

Galatians 2:19-21
For through the law I died to the law, so that I might live to God. I have been crucified with Christ; and it is no longer I who live, but it is Christ who lives in me. And the life I now live in the flesh I live by faith in the Son of God, who loved me and gave himself for me. I do not nullify the grace of God; for if justification comes through the law, then Christ died for nothing.

❖ ❖ ❖

There is nothing more necessary than grace for the Christian life. There is nothing more difficult to grasp than grace. We understand the rule of law. We know what it means to make a law, break a law, enforce a law. We understand that those who disobey the law should be punished and those who obey the law should be rewarded because obedience is no small feat. But we know that we cannot function without grace, and yet we stumble in understanding it, and worse yet, we fail completely at offering it to others. The cross of Jesus Christ is, among many things, a reminder to us that the grace we have been given and that we have to give is not to be taken for granted.

❖ ❖ ❖

Gracious God, forgive the thoughtlessness of our self-absorbed lives. Amen.

JULY ◆ 16

Luke 7:47
Therefore, I tell you, her sins, which were many, have been forgiven; hence she has shown great love. But the one to whom little is forgiven, loves little."

❖   ❖   ❖

One of the lessons I taught confirmands was called "Who needs a savior?" We spent a few minutes looking at the stories in the headlines of the newspaper and it didn't take long to conclude that the world needs a savior. The more difficult step was accepting that WE need a savior. We are quick in our relationships to justify our actions, defend our motives, explain our mistakes. We do it with our friends and family and with God. The hurt feelings linger even though it may all be perfectly understandable. Great love happens not when we defend ourselves but when we trust in the power of forgiveness. We, who need a Savior, know what it means to be forgiven, what it means be loved.

❖   ❖   ❖

Holy God, help us to forgive often and love much. Amen.

JULY ◆ 17

John 4: 6
Jesus, tired out by his journey, was sitting by the well.

❖   ❖   ❖

In the early years of the Christian faith, there were those who believed that Jesus was truly God, but not human. When difficulties arise in matters of faith sometimes those who mean well seek to remove the obstacle, but in the process often harm the whole. If Jesus was not truly human then he might not have felt hunger or pain. The thorns pressed onto his head would not hurt like it would us. The cross was just a passage and not a real death. But those, like John, who traveled with Jesus witnessed his hunger and his agony. We need a God who is God & bigger than we can imagine, greater in wisdom and justice than anything we can create. We also need a God who understands a sleepless night, a blister, a broken heart. Such a God may be too big for us to wrap our heads around and believe, but anything less than a God who understands our weariness would be no God at all.

❖   ❖   ❖

Lord God, enter into our humanity and redeem it so that it may shine as you intended. Amen.

JULY ◆ 18

Isaiah 65:1-2
I was ready to be sought out by those who did not ask, to be found by those who did not seek me. I said, "Here I am, here I am," to a nation that did not call on my name. I held out my hands all day long to a rebellious people, who walk in a way that is not good, following their own devices

❖ ❖ ❖

I believe that it was Mark Twain who imagined the metaphor for raising teenagers as sending them through a long, translucent tunnel and all the parents could do is beat on the glass, shout muffled words of guidance and warning, and hope that they come out of the tunnel into their adulthood alive. Some parents might choose to bypass the tunnel but eventually youth must become adults. If we do not grant them freedom within limits along the way, they will either delay their adulthood or demand freedom in such a way as to damage the relationship. This is how we are wired. We cherish freedom and independence but we still need grace for our relationships to survive our selfishness. Had God wanted puppets for family, he would have made us with strings attached. With the freedom we are given as children of God, we can lean into wise guidance and love or rebelliously turn away. God shows us his character by giving us the choice.

❖ ❖ ❖

Lord God, may we move through this day without making you have to work so hard. Amen.

July ◆ 19

John 6:27
Do not work for the food that perishes, but for the food that endures for eternal life, which the Son of Man will give you.

❖   ❖   ❖

I learned about the four values levels that provide motivation for all that we do. The first level is personal - "I do this work well because it makes me feel good." The second level is organizational - "I do this work well because it makes money for my whole household." The third level is identity - "I do this work well so that it will bring honor to my whole community." The fourth level is overriding purpose – "I do this work well to glorify God." There are days, even minutes of those days, in which we are operating on various levels, sometimes depending on the task. The tedious things that just need to be done don't immediately motivate me. Reaching to a higher value always helps. There is something about the joy of working for the sake of others - especially God - that gives us stamina that we didn't know we had.

❖   ❖   ❖

Let everything we do today, O Lord, be done for you. Amen.

JULY ◆ 20

Galatians 3:27-28
As many of you as were baptized into Christ have clothed yourselves with Christ. There is no longer Jew or Greek, there is no longer slave or free, there is no longer male and female; for all of you are one in Christ Jesus.

❖ ❖ ❖

Paul could not have picked three more daunting walls that have stood strong and been more fiercely protected than that of ethnicity, economic status, and gender. Hot and cold wars have been fought to maintain those barriers. The possibility of any unity has been left waste in the defensive rubble. The cross of Christ is the great equalizer. In the death of a genuine human, the things which we guard as our identity fade away in the light of love at its purest power.

❖ ❖ ❖

Holy God, reduce us to the most common denominator that we might serve others in your most holy name. Amen.

JULY ◆ 21

Luke 8:37-39
Then all the people of the surrounding country of the Gerasenes asked Jesus to leave them; for they were seized with great fear. So he got into the boat and returned. The man from whom the demons had gone begged that he might be with him; but Jesus sent him away, saying, "Return to your home, and declare how much God has done for you." So he went away, proclaiming throughout the city how much Jesus had done for him.

❖ ❖ ❖

A man possessed by demons for years was less frightening to the people than Jesus. Jesus rocked their world. They had been familiar with demons and disease and sin. They were not at all accustomed to health and wholeness. They asked Jesus to leave. The man wanted to leave with him. Jesus asked the man to stay behind so that he could be a daily, living witness to the power of God. We have a choice to make too. Either we embrace the power of God at work in our lives and in the world, or we are afraid of it and push it away.

❖ ❖ ❖

Be patient with us, O Lord, as we push and pull. Amen.

JULY ◆ 22

I Kings 19:19-20
So he set out from there, and found Elisha son of Shaphat, who was plowing. There were twelve yoke of oxen ahead of him, and he was with the twelfth. Elijah passed by him and threw his mantle over him. He left the oxen, ran after Elijah, and said, "Let me kiss my father and my mother, and then I will follow you."

❖   ❖   ❖

We would like to think that more deliberate thought went into choosing the next prophet of God for the people of Israel than picking the 12th yoke of oxen in field. But what if there wasn't any more thought in it than that. Elisha was not chosen for his brilliant rhetoric, his sterling character, or his sparkling resume. Perhaps he was chosen randomly out of a field not to show how great Elisha was but the nature of the greatest of God. Perhaps God needed more people who would rely on him completely rather than rest on their laurels.

❖   ❖   ❖

Holy God, may we be your servants this day as we lean on you. Amen.

JULY ◆ 23

Psalm 16:1-2
Protect me, O God, for in you I take refuge. I say to the Lord, "You are my Lord; I have no good apart from you."

❖   ❖   ❖

One of the aspects of marriage that I have come to learn through listening to many couples is that marriage gives people an opportunity to be seen by another human being at one's best and one's worst. The worst is always a given, but a healthy relationship is one in which the best is brought out in powerful and sometimes courageous ways. God gives us the opportunity to be our best and forgives us our worst. It isn't any wonder why marriage at its best is still the best earthly example of our relationship with God.

❖   ❖   ❖

Holy God, bring out the best in who we are so that the world will know your mercy and love. Amen.

JULY ◆ 24

Psalm 34:1-3
I will bless the Lord at all times; his praise shall continually be in my mouth. My soul makes its boast in the Lord; let the humble hear and be glad. O magnify the Lord with me, and let us exalt his name together.

❖ ❖ ❖

When I first became aware of how much the Lord loved the world and started to get a real look at the magnitude of his grace, I thought, 'Why do we Christians work so hard at keeping this a secret?' I am not talking about the noisy ones who spew religious phrases like diluted fruit punch in conversations. I am talking about those who have walked through some dark, awful places and can look over our shoulders at the power of God to save us from ourselves. If we are not vibrating with thanksgiving every day, then we perhaps need to stop and take one breath, feel it fill our lungs and permeate our bodies, and then take another breath and receive it for what it is - a gift, God's CPR. And then with that breath we breathe out the word, "Thank you." And we keep doing it until we mean it. We need to breath out the secret that the God who gave us life is still on the job.

❖ ❖ ❖

Every breath I take, Lord, is filled with your love. Thank you, Thank you. Amen.

JULY ◆ 25

Luke 9:57-58
As they were going along the road, someone said to him, "I will follow you wherever you go." And Jesus said to him, "Foxes have holes, and birds of the air have nests; but the Son of Man has nowhere to lay his head."

❖ ❖ ❖

Jesus had made the turn toward Jerusalem where he would be arrested, beaten, and killed. The last few years of his life had been spent on the road, rarely staying in one place long. Sometimes he stayed in the homes of others and sometimes he slept by a campfire or in a boat. Just as well that he didn't have a house. We would have made a museum of it with tour guides and a gift shop. To follow Jesus is not about honoring his legacy or his memory. To follow Jesus is to walk toward our cross on a Gospel road that begs for travelers propelled forward by the power of redeeming love.

❖ ❖ ❖

Day by Day, O Dear Lord, three things I pray - to see thee more clearly, love thee more dearly, follow thee more nearly. Amen.

JULY ◆ 26

John 6:65-69
And he said, "For this reason I have told you that no one can come to me unless it is granted by the Father." Because of this many of his disciples turned back and no longer went about with him. So Jesus asked the twelve, "Do you also wish to go away?" Simon Peter answered him, "Lord, to whom can we go? You have the words of eternal life. We have come to believe and know that you are the Holy One of God."

❖   ❖   ❖

I wonder what that must have been like for the twelve disciples to watch others turn their backs and leave. The Gospels reveal to us that the twelve disciples did not suddenly have a deep and profound conviction of faith in Christ as the Savior of the World. That conviction grew over time. It was not without missteps, fear, deep doubt, and outright failure. There are days when I want to do more than just turn my back and walk away - I want to run screaming from the room. As a child, I remember running away from home one day and getting a few blocks down the road on my bike until it dawned on me that I didn't know where I was going. I was smart enough, at least, to know that my options were limited. As difficult, as challenging, as confusing, as frightening, as messy as it is to be a follower of Jesus Christ, it still beats chasing my own tail.

❖   ❖   ❖

Holy God, surround your people when we want to run away so that wherever we go, we run to you. Amen.

JULY ◆ 27

Hosea 6:4-6
What shall I do with you, O Ephraim? What shall I do with you, O Judah? Your love is like a morning cloud, like the dew that goes away early. Therefore I have hewn them by the prophets, I have killed them by the words of my mouth, and my judgment goes forth as the light. For I desire steadfast love and not sacrifice, the knowledge of God rather than burnt offerings.

❖ ❖ ❖

"What shall I do with you?" It seems to be the phrase most often uttered by parents in an out loud sigh. It is one of those phrases that grant us a moment to think and not react in anger. We have a second inside that sigh and at the end of that question to choose a course of action that is born of wisdom and not total frustration. God sighed over us time and time again. God's purposes are driven by love. Though capable of being frustrated, our Lord still chooses to love us through the frustration.

❖ ❖ ❖

Holy God, thank you for your patience through the times we frustrate you. Amen.

JULY ◆ 28

Philippians 4:8
Finally, beloved, whatever is true, whatever is honorable, whatever is just, whatever is pure, whatever is pleasing, whatever is commendable, if there is any excellence and if there is anything worthy of praise, think about these things.

❖ ❖ ❖

Some years ago when I was caught up in a vortex of negative stuff, a good friend told me to read this passage over and over and over again until I became aware of truth, honor, justice, excellence around me. It felt like a physical exercise, at first. When things go wrong, it is easy to see other things going wrong. The attitude is like an undertow that you never see coming until it is sucking the life out of you. It is work to pull against that current. To walk as children of the light instead of skulking about in the darkness is to take baby steps. It is doing remedial schooling in the meaning of praise-worthy things. The next step is to see what is pleasing and to do it. By the grace of God, it can be done. There is joy in them, thar hills.

❖ ❖ ❖

Holy God, help us to turn our attention away from the shadows into your marvelous light. Amen.

July ◆ 29

Romans 4:23-25
Now the words, "it was reckoned to him," were written not for his sake alone, but for ours also. It will be reckoned to us who believe in him who raised Jesus our Lord from the dead, who was handed over to death for our trespasses and was raised for our justification.

❖   ❖   ❖

I used to work near a small, privately owned clothing store in a little town. The owner was called "Judge Keller" because he and his father before him could judge the pant size of anyone walking into their shop. Shopping there was an experience of clothing filled bins, streams of light, creaking and uneven wooden floors, and the musty smell of wood and wool. In the end, the Judge would calculate the bill with a black marker on the side of a brown paper sack and he would also ask you to "check his figures." The clothes I purchased there are long since gone but the gift of that paper sack experience still lingers. When God is calculating the cost of our sin, he figures in the death of his Son. Somewhere in the miracle of God's math, we walk out with our lives, with freedom, with love beyond anything we will ever deserve....a miracle in a brown wrapper.

❖   ❖   ❖

Holy God, for the grace of your arithmetic, we give you our lives. Amen.

JULY ◆ 30

Hebrews 10:5-7
Consequently, when Christ came into the world, he said, "Sacrifices and offerings you have not desired, but a body you have prepared for me; in burnt offerings and sin offerings you have taken no pleasure. Then I said, "See, God, I have come to do your will, O God."

❖ ❖ ❖

We spend a lot of time and energy trying to make up for the mistakes we make. We work a little harder around the house. We try to make it up to our friends. We buy a little gift to make amends. Most times, it actually works enough that we continue to buy the gift or make the gesture. Sometimes it doesn't cut it. And it definitely doesn't cut it when it comes to our relationship with God. When will we understand that we can experience the fullness of the gift of our lives not through bargaining for God's love? What pleases God is an open and grateful heart.

❖ ❖ ❖

Lord God, for the offering of your Son so that we may know life, we give you thanks. Amen.

JULY ◆ 31

Luke 3:1-2
In the fifteenth year of the reign of Emperor Tiberius, when Pontius Pilate was governor of Judea, and Herod was ruler of Galilee, and his brother Philip ruler of the region of Ituraea and Trachonitis, and Lysanias ruler of Abilene, during the high priesthood of Annas and Caiaphas, the word of God came to John son of Zechariah in the wilderness.

❖   ❖   ❖

In a Peanuts cartoon, Charlie Brown found Linus reading a Russian novel. Charlie Brown asked him how he could manage to wade through all the complicated foreign names. Linus shrugged and said, "Oh, I just blurb over them." Linus' advice helped me appreciate the Russian novels I had to read in college. Most of the time, it is all right to do the same with the strange sounding names in the scriptures - just blurb over them. There are times, however, when those names were placed in the text intentionally like a quilter uses ties or stitches to anchor the layers of cloth together. The events leading up to the birth of Jesus Christ are purposefully anchored in human history with names of leaders so that all would know that era and place and moment when God entered human history for the salvation of the world. When we wrap our heads around those strange sounding names, we touch the thread of swaddling clothes, the tunic of a carpenter, and the robe of a king.

❖   ❖   ❖

Master Designer, may we be woven into your gracious design for the world. Amen.

AUGUST ◆ 1

Exodus 19:4-6
You have seen what I did to the Egyptians, and how I bore you on eagles' wings and brought you to myself. Now therefore, if you obey my voice and keep my covenant, you shall be my treasured possession out of all the peoples. Indeed, the whole earth is mine, but you shall be for me a priestly kingdom and a holy nation. These are the words that you shall speak to the Israelites."

❖ ❖ ❖

One of the advantages of growing older (and there are advantages....really!) is that we have collected over the years examples of God's grace, mercy and power. When the nation of Israel was just being established, they didn't have a long history in their relationship with God. But God had freed them from slavery, preserved them from plagues, and provided a pathway through the Red Sea. With this one memory told over and over again through their history, each generation learned about the trustworthiness of God's promises. In our own life times, we have experienced the grace of God in a thousand different ways. God is at work today. Look for it.

❖ ❖ ❖

Holy God, for the witness of the countless times in which you have cared for us, we give you thanks. Amen.

AUGUST ◆ 2

Psalm 100:4-5
Enter his gates with thanksgiving, and his courts with praise. Give thanks to him, bless his name. For the Lord is good; his steadfast love endures forever, and his faithfulness to all generations.

❖   ❖   ❖

My prayers rarely start with praise and thanksgiving. The first word out of my mouth is more likely "Help!" than anything else. I heard a doctor recently refer to the over-the-counter pain relievers as "rescue drugs." They help in the moment with the common aches and pains. We often treat God like a rescue drug. Like any loving parent, God is at the ready for us. I imagine, however, it would be a refreshing change of pace in our prayers once in a while to share our excitement that God is exactly who God claims to be.

❖   ❖   ❖

Great to be with you, Lord! Amen!

AUGUST ♦ 3

Romans 5:1-5
Therefore, since we are justified by faith, we have peace with God through our Lord Jesus Christ, through whom we have obtained access to this grace in which we stand; and we boast in our hope of sharing the glory of God. And not only that, but we also boast in our sufferings, knowing that suffering produces endurance, and endurance produces character, and character produces hope, and hope does not disappoint us, because God's love has been poured into our hearts through the Holy Spirit that has been given to us.

❖ ❖ ❖

There are types of adhesive products that come in separate containers. They have to be mixed together and used in the moment for the two ingredients to work effectively. We have a tremendous capacity for hope which is born of suffering, character, and endurance. At the same time, however, we have known deep disappointment and crushed hope. There is, thankfully, the active ingredient of God's love which activates our inert and vulnerable hope turning it into an indomitable force.

❖ ❖ ❖

God of hope, stir us into strong disciples and hopeful servants. Amen.

AUGUST ◆ 4

Matthew 9:11-14
Whatever town or village you enter, find out who in it is worthy, and stay there until you leave. As you enter the house, greet it. If the house is worthy, let your peace come upon it; but if it is not worthy, let your peace return to you. If anyone will not welcome you or listen to your words, shake off the dust from your feet as you leave that house or town.

❖ ❖ ❖

As awkward and frustrating as it is at times, we must come to grips with the fact that we are called into mission to share the Gospel of Jesus Christ with others. We believe the Holy Spirit works in lives to stir people to faith and service. We are to share relentlessly and trust that God will work his will in his time and way. Walking away from a "house" that is not receptive or willing to listen is one of the more difficult things I have ever done. The longer you linger, the longer the dust of that house not only settles on your feet, it gets under your skin and it is breathed into your lungs and that house becomes a part of who you are. To move on to a place that will be more welcoming is more complicated and painful than shaking the dust off one's feet. It requires open-heart surgery. And still we are called to keep moving and tell the story to whoever will listen.

❖ ❖ ❖

Holy God, give us the grace to know when to linger and when to move. Amen.

AUGUST ◆ 5

Jeremiah 20:7-9
O Lord, you have enticed me, and I was enticed; you have overpowered me, and you have prevailed. I have become a laughing stock all day long; everyone mocks me. For whenever I speak, I must cry out, I must shout, "Violence and destruction!" For the word of the Lord has become for me a reproach and derision all day long. If I say, "I will not mention him, or speak any more in his name," then within me there is something like a burning fire shut up in my bones; I am weary with holding it in, and I cannot.

❖ ❖ ❖

Jeremiah had the unenviable task of telling the people that they were wrong, that they needed to repent and change their ways. For his obedience to the Lord, he was rebuffed, abused and isolated. Jeremiah thought that just giving up the message would ease his pain, but he was compelled from the inside out to continue in the task God had given him to do. When we try to stifle the prophetic voice that calls us away from sin and toward the will of God, we only hurt ourselves. We become a part of the problem. The responsibility in a relationship to confront one another is one from which we all often run, but no good purpose is served in the running except for a temporary and false sense of peace. We dive into these confrontations with the hope that God will bless the effort, forgive the messiness of the process, and send us out more whole than when we started.

❖ ❖ ❖

Holy God, help us to listen to the prophets who come to us and help us be a prophetic voice with courage. Amen.

AUGUST ◆ 6

Psalm 69:12-14
I am the subject of gossip for those who sit in the gate, and the drunkards make songs about me. But as for me, my prayer is to you, O Lord. At an acceptable time, O God, in the abundance of your steadfast love, answer me. With your faithful help rescue me from sinking in the mire; let me be delivered from my enemies and from the deep waters.

❖   ❖   ❖

It is a simple truth. Children will mimic their parents. They will make their sandwich like they have seen sandwiches made. They shout out a frustrated curse word even before they are old enough to know it is a curse word. As we struggle in our faith, which we all do, we are to be mindful of those who are watching us and learning from us. Even in the pit, we are to remind ourselves that we are not alone. We are to remember that there is no pit where God is not. We are to crawl, if necessary, and learn to walk again. We are challenged to live a grateful life and not to participate with those who gossip at the gate or revel in the misfortunes of others. We witness even in our struggles to another way of life.

❖   ❖   ❖

Thank you, Lord, thank you. Amen.

AUGUST ◆ 7

Romans 6:9-11
We know that Christ, being raised from the dead, will never die again; death no longer has dominion over him. The death he died, he died to sin, once for all; but the life he lives, he lives to God. So you also must consider yourselves dead to sin and alive to God in Christ Jesus.

❖ ❖ ❖

Dead or alive. Those two possibilities were never really a matter of choice. What Christ did on the cross for the sake of the world was to give us the freedom to choose to die to sin and the freedom to choose to live in the name of Christ. At least once during the day, I bark myself to "Focus!" I need to focus on the task at hand, on the person in front of me with a problem or a question, or on the presence of God in the moment. It takes some effort because the signs of death often overwhelm the signs of life. We are the most important sign of life witnessing to God's grace. We are dead to sin and alive to God. There is no more freeing thought on which we could focus.

❖ ❖ ❖

Holy God, grant us a vision of life today that can overwhelm the darkness of sin. Amen.

AUGUST ◆ 8

Matthew 10:29
Are not two sparrows sold for a penny? Yet not one of them will fall to the ground apart from your Father.

❖   ❖   ❖

We continue to need constant reminders that we are worth something. In a world of billions of people, most of whom have it much worse off than we do; we are sucked into the vortex of a culture that turns humans into productivity devices. We are left to assume that we have no worth in the scheme of things or to do whatever we think we need to do to be worthwhile. So we are reminded of a God who is larger than we can imagine. A God whose imagination spans the universe. A God who attends to the details with compassion and energy. We are reminded that we are, indeed, one of many details to which God attends and we don't have to do anything but acknowledge our own worth. And if we want to do something, perhaps our neighbors could use a reminder that they are valuable, too.

❖   ❖   ❖

Holy God, hear our prayer and give us the faith to believe in our worth in your eyes. Amen.

AUGUST ◆ 9

Isaiah 35:6-7
Then the lame shall leap like a deer, and the tongue of the speechless sing for joy. For the waters shall break forth in the wilderness, and streams in the desert; the burning sand shall become a pool, and the thirsty ground springs of water.

❖ ❖ ❖

To the people of God who were weak in the face of strong oppression, the prophet's words of hope were like a drink of cool water on a hot day. The vision of people made whole and thirst quenched is a tangible image of a God who cares intimately for us. Sometimes even in the midst of some dry times, we can drink the words of promise and find satisfaction in the taste of hope.

❖ ❖ ❖

Holy God, stir the waters of hope and strength so that we can meet the challenges of the day. Amen.

AUGUST ◆ 10

Zechariah 9:11-12
As for you also, because of the blood of my covenant with you, I will set your prisoners free from the waterless pit. Return to your stronghold, O prisoners of hope; today I declare that I will restore to you double.

❖ ❖ ❖

In ancient deserts of Biblical times, deep pits were dug for the collection of water. A dry pit was handy place to throw someone if you needed a swift prison facility. At summer camp, we were all given water bottles and told every day to have full bottles with us at all times. Even still, people got sick from dehydration. We are our own waterless pit. We hold in our hands what we need and still we forget. When we return to the promises of our baptism, we are invited to drink in the grace and mercy we need to live abundantly.

❖ ❖ ❖

Holy God, for the gift of water, for the word of life, for the power of hope, we give you thanks. Amen.

August ◆ 11

I Kings 5:13-14
But his servants approached and said to him, "Father, if the prophet had commanded you to do something difficult, would you not have done it? How much more, when all he said to you was, 'Wash, and be clean'?" So he went down and immersed himself seven times in the Jordan, according to the word of the man of God; his flesh was restored like the flesh of a young boy, and he was clean.

❖ ❖ ❖

I was told once by a personnel recruiter that the kiss of death phrase on a potential employee's recommendation form is "lacks common sense." After having to channel surf through too many news channels covering the pouting Hollywood celebrities or hundreds of people waiting in line for days so that they can be the first to spend hundreds of dollars for a gadget that will be out of style in months, I have my doubts about our collective common sense. In the scripture lesson, a king with leprosy has an opportunity for healing that requires little effort and no cost but he balks because it isn't done instantly for him. Fortunately he was surrounded by servants who did not lack common sense or the courage and compassion for their master to tell him what he needed to hear. When we are being propelled by our own foolishness, God surrounds us with a cloud of witnesses to guide us if we are willing to listen.

❖ ❖ ❖

Holy God, may we be wise enough to listen and courageous enough to speak so that all may know of your grace. Amen.

AUGUST ◆ 12

Psalm 66:16-19
Come and hear, all you who fear God, and I will tell what he has done for me. I cried aloud to him, and he was extolled with my tongue. If I had cherished iniquity in my heart, the Lord would not have listened. But truly God has listened; he has given heed to the words of my prayer.

❖ ❖ ❖

Let's face it. We all want attention. We want to be understood. We want to be accepted for who we are. We want our needs, at the very least, regarded and acknowledged. We want to know that our existence matters to someone. In a very need-driven culture, we attend to the needy ones but we develop bad habits when we are the ones needing the attention of those who understand us. We pout or explode or redirect our frustration on an innocent victim or we hurt ourselves. Children are expected to ask for help. Adults are expected to take care of themselves. In our relationship with God we are given the freedom - no matter our age - to be a child who can freely ask for attention. The miracle is that even before we utter our first pitiful whimper of "No one cares about me" - the Master of the Universe is listening.

❖ ❖ ❖

Holy God, thank you for making your lap so inviting and your arms so big and your ears so willing to listen. Amen.

AUGUST ◆ 13

Deuteronomy 30:11,14
Surely, this commandment that I am commanding you today is not too hard for you, nor is it too far away..... No, the word is very near to you; it is in your mouth and in your heart for you to observe.

❖   ❖   ❖

Martin Luther spent long months in small, drafty room of a German fortress translating the Bible into the German language so that his country people could read the scriptures for themselves. But centuries later, with a plethora of translations at our fingertips, there is a growing virus of Biblical illiteracy among those of us who push the scriptures away for reasons of it being too difficult, too confusing, too culturally obscure, too irrelevant. But God made what is essential in scripture clear and accessible. We have within us - the Spirit of the Living God - what we need to read, understand, and respond with obedience to the Word of God.

❖   ❖   ❖

Holy God, thank you for your word that continues to be refreshment for our souls. Amen.

AUGUST ◆ 14

Psalm 25:5-7
Lead me in your truth, and teach me, for you are the God of my salvation; for you I wait all day long. Be mindful of your mercy, O Lord, and of your steadfast love, for they have been from of old. Do not remember the sins of my youth or my transgressions; according to your steadfast love remember me, for your goodness' sake, O Lord!

❖   ❖   ❖

Most embarrassing moments....everyone has them and everyone remembers them. No matter how much our capacity to remember details diminishes our worst memories still land in the present relentlessly. We want God to see us at our best but our worst always floats to the surface. There was a movie about Alzheimer's disease called "Do you remember love?" The miracle of God's character is that he can choose to forget our sins and remember us according to his steadfast love. God remembers love and it always knows our name.

❖   ❖   ❖

Holy God, thank you for choosing to love us through our worst and best. Amen.

AUGUST ◆ 15

Colossian 1:7-8
This you learned from Epaphras, our beloved fellow servant. He is a faithful minister of Christ on your behalf, and he has made known to us your love in the Spirit.

❖   ❖   ❖

One could wish for such words to be used to described oneself: "our, beloved, fellow, servant, faithful, minister." Epaphras is little known. He was a minor character in a life-sized drama and yet he is known by the relationships that were the fabric of his life. The only deed he is known for actually doing is to have carried a message to Paul of the spirited love of the Colossians. Epaphras witnessed to the world of the importance of lifting one another up for the sake of the Gospel. We were meant to be woven together and we honor the God who loves us when we attend to the threads.

❖   ❖   ❖

Holy God, for the work you have given us to do and for the people with whom we do the work....we give you thanks, Amen.

AUGUST ◆ 16

Psalm 145:13-14
Your kingdom is an everlasting kingdom, and your dominion endures throughout all generations. The Lord is faithful in all his words, and gracious in all his deeds. The Lord upholds all who are falling, and raises up all who are bowed down.

❖ ❖ ❖

Gas prices are often in the news because they affect a wide spectrum of the economy. We are more acutely aware than ever of how a price increase in one arena forces up prices in another. Charitable organizations feel the economic pinch and are often forced to make painful choices in services even as needs grow. Changes in cultural priorities from one generation to the next tear at the fabric of our lives together. Now more than ever, we feel the need for continuity, balance, and hope. Ancient, faithful ones witness to a God who continues to keep his promises amid the craziness of human fluctuations. God's economy evens the playing field so that those who feel the burden of deep need are lifted up.

❖ ❖ ❖

Holy God, may we be this day champions for your message of hope to all the generations. Amen.

AUGUST ◆ 17

Romans 7:18-20
For I know that nothing good dwells within me, that is, in my flesh. I can will what is right, but I cannot do it. For I do not do the good I want, but the evil I do not want is what I do. Now if I do what I do not want, it is no longer I that do it, but sin that dwells within me.

❖   ❖   ❖

The culture in which the Apostle Paul wrote was heavily influenced by Greek philosophy which often explained the nature of human character in dual terms: flesh and spirit, evil and good, mind and heart. Variations on the philosophies put a greater value on one over the other - usually the flesh was evil and the spirit good. Along comes Jesus who is both God and Man, body and soul, but he is all good. Jesus is what God intended for us as human beings - a whole person at peace inside their own skin and at peace in their relationship with God. It is sin that makes our skin crawl and turns us on ourselves and anyone who would make our lives even more uncomfortable. Paul is laying out a way of thinking that will help us acknowledge that we need saving and that we can't save ourselves. Even if we could imagine a wonderful blueprint of salvation, we could never build it. Over and over again, day after day, the voice of our savior beckons to us. "Take my hand."

❖   ❖   ❖

Sinful as we are, Lord, you love us stubbornly. May we be less reluctant to admit that we need you. Amen.

AUGUST ◆ 18

Matthew 11:28-30
"Come to me, all you that are weary and are carrying heavy burdens, and I will give you rest. Take my yoke upon you, and learn from me; for I am gentle and humble in heart, and you will find rest for your souls. For my yoke is easy, and my burden is light."

❖ ❖ ❖

This is one of those verses that slows us down and immediately makes us want to crawl into that friendly, empty space being offered to us. It immediately recognizes our weariness and our burdens and extends words that even of themselves are healing: rest, gentle, humble, easy, light. One of the greatest compliments I have ever heard is "You make room for other people in the conversation." It is a simple thing and yet as we move through our days too busy and full of ourselves, it is not a simple task to make room. Jesus extends to us an open hand, a place to lay burdens down and a way in which we can both find rest and a new purpose. Giving one another that kind of space requires that we are not so burdened that we cannot create space for one another to rediscover the Savior who emptied himself for us.

❖ ❖ ❖

In the shelter of your heart, Lord, may we learn to make space for others. Amen.

AUGUST ◆ 19

Isaiah 55:6-7
Seek the Lord while he may be found, call upon him while he is near; let the wicked forsake their way, and the unrighteous their thoughts; let them return to the Lord, that he may have mercy on them, and to our God, for he will abundantly pardon.

❖   ❖   ❖

The Lord spent more time chasing after the people who had broken their promises to God than God ever spent making those promises. The grace of the Old Testament is best viewed with a wide screen. God promises. The people cheer. Time passes. The people forget. The people sin. God gets angry, punishes, and gives the people the promise again. That is repeated throughout the history of the people of Israel. Christ finally fulfills the law and establishes a new covenant, a new promise - eternal life and forgiveness of sins. We are called to live not so much perfectly as gratefully.

❖   ❖   ❖

Holy God, may we learn this day the power of living thankfully. Amen.

AUGUST ◆ 20

Psalm 65:6-8
By your strength you established the mountains; you are girded with might. You silence the roaring of the seas, the roaring of their waves, the tumult of the peoples. Those who live at earth's farthest bounds are awed by your signs; you make the gateways of the morning and the evening shout for joy.

❖ ❖ ❖

I once stayed in a hotel that faced the ocean on the Oregon coast. The view out my window was spectacular. The waves crashing on the magnificent rock formations were a gift of one beautiful photograph after the other particularly at sunset and sunrise. When it was time for bed, however, the sound was relentless, pounding, violent, and I foolishly thought it would shut itself off for the night as if it were a laborer on a time clock. Being reminded from time to time who made the mountains and who owns the switch on the ocean surf is not a bad thing. It is enough to quiet the tumult even in a single soul.

❖ ❖ ❖

Holy God, quiet the noise of our anxious hearts and help us to find rest inside your enormous will. Amen.

AUGUST ◆ 21

Romans 8:1-2
There is therefore now no condemnation for those who are in Christ Jesus. For the law of the Spirit of life in Christ Jesus has set you free from the law of sin and of death.

❖   ❖   ❖

There is a world of hurt that never ceases to stun me as I talk with people. We don't have to scratch too deeply beyond the veneer of normalcy to discover pain upon pain that is wreaking havoc with our bones and our families and our culture. It is a rare person who has not known rejection and criticism that diminishes us even more. No slick television talk show guest or self-help book can give us a sustaining conviction of our own worth. We try to wash our own brains with a truth that we dream but can't make real. Through the haze of our own foolishness comes the voice of the one who sets us free from our own prison.

❖   ❖   ❖

This day, Lord, may we believe you are telling us the truth, that you are God, that we need you and that you love us. Amen.

AUGUST ◆ 22

Matthew 13:15-17
For this people's heart has grown dull, and their ears are hard of hearing, and they have shut their eyes; so that they might not look with their eyes, and listen with their ears, and understand with their heart and turn- and I would heal them.' But blessed are your eyes, for they see, and your ears, for they hear. Truly I tell you, many prophets and righteous people longed to see what you see, but did not see it, and to hear what you hear, but did not hear it.

❖ ❖ ❖

One of greatest challenges in the Christian community is convincing people that their faith needs to grow. We make changes in our lives from the time we were children to now. We change our perspectives on what is important. We alter spending habits. We mature in our relationships with other people. Too often we are content to leave our faith rolling around on the floor of a Sunday School room somewhere in our distant past. We acknowledge God. We pray in a pinch. We attend church when we are able and call it good. And it is all good, but God offers us so much more that not to nurture our faith throughout adulthood is to live half a life.

❖ ❖ ❖

Holy God, deepen our faith with a hunger to know you better. Amen.

AUGUST ◆ 23

Isaiah 55:1-2
Ho, everyone who thirsts, come to the waters; and you that have no money, come, buy and eat! Come, buy wine and milk without money and without price. Why do you spend your money for that which is not bread, and your labor for that which does not satisfy? Listen carefully to me, and eat what is good, and delight yourselves in rich food.

❖   ❖   ❖

Why is it that we have to be coaxed, cajoled, and persuaded to do something that is good for us? Probably because we have learned not to trust. We have been told that a certain food is good for us but have learned that means it doesn't taste great. The person who invites us to swim because the "water is fine" really wants us to discover how cold it is. The salesperson selling us something is after the sale first above our best interest. When we are invited by God's people to enter more deeply into a relationship with God we continue to be naturally suspicious. As in any relationship, we must move and live by faith. We can't live without trusting something even if it means trusting our guts. The spirit of the living God lives in those guts inviting us to take that leap of faith in God's direction.

❖   ❖   ❖

Holy God, we believe that what you desire is a relationship with us and that what you want for us is better than we can imagine. Amen.

AUGUST ◆ 24

Psalm 145:14-18
The Lord upholds all who are falling, and raises up all who are bowed down. The eyes of all look to you, and you give them their food in due season. You open your hand, satisfying the desire of every living thing. The Lord is just in all his ways, and kind in all his doings. The Lord is near to all who call on him, to all who call on him in truth.

❖ ❖ ❖

There is a song that says, "I need a hero I'm holding out for a hero 'til the end of the night. He's gotta be strong and he's gotta be fast and he's gotta be fresh from the fight. I need a hero I'm holding out for a hero 'til the morning light He's gotta be sure and it's gotta be soon and he's gotta be larger than life." The psalmist captures our age-old hunger for a Lord bigger than we can imagine and strong enough to hold us together. What is mind boggling is that when we join God in the mission to uphold, raise up, feed, satisfy, and love, we find the hero that God is by the power of making us heroic for the sake of others.

❖ ❖ ❖

Holy God, give us the strength this day to trust that you are holding us so that we can reach beyond ourselves. Amen.

AUGUST ◆ 25

Romans 9:1-3
I am speaking the truth in Christ-I am not lying; my conscience confirms it by the Holy Spirit- I have great sorrow and unceasing anguish in my heart. For I could wish that I myself were accursed and cut off from Christ for the sake of my own people, my kindred according to the flesh.

❖ ❖ ❖

Paul, a former champion for the Hebrew faith, agonized for those who were not convinced as he was that Jesus was the long-awaited Messiah. Waiting had become such a way of life, it was hard to imagine that the wait was over. Generations had waited. Other false messiahs had come and gone. Who was to say that this Jesus was not one of them? The power of Paul's witness could only find a home in a hungry heart, one which was willing to step boldly into an undiscovered country. Paul could not help but go where he was compelled by the truth he knew and call out to those he so longed to have on the journey with him.

❖ ❖ ❖

Precious Lord, help us to be relentless in our invitation to those who wander in their own wilderness. Amen.

AUGUST ◆ 26

Matthew 14:16-21
Jesus said to them, "They need not go away; you give them something to eat." They replied, "We have nothing here but five loaves and two fish." And he said, "Bring them here to me." Then he ordered the crowds to sit down on the grass. Taking the five loaves and the two fish, he looked up to heaven, and blessed and broke the loaves, and gave them to the disciples, and the disciples gave them to the crowds. And all ate and were filled; and they took up what was left over of the broken pieces, twelve baskets full. And those who ate were about five thousand men, besides women and children.

❖   ❖   ❖

Luther said in a sermon that when the Bethlehem innkeeper reported to Mary and Joseph that there were no rooms in the inn, he lied. Luther's point was that there were ALL the rooms in the inn. We are so like the innkeeper in Bethlehem saying there are no rooms or the disciples saying we have nothing to feed the crowd. We have the room and the food. What we need is the will to let go and share what we have. Some are motivated by the warm feeling of a philanthropic gesture. Some are motivated by compassion. Some are motivated by a deep awareness of what has been given to them. Some are not motivated until they can be convinced that their gift will not be squandered or unappreciated. Some are not motivated at all. While we ponder the problems with our motivation to care for the poor, the poor are still hungry and Jesus is praying for us.

❖   ❖   ❖

Lord God, bless what we have so that we may see how easily it could be shared. Amen.

AUGUST ◆ 27

Psalm 19:14
Let the words of my mouth and the meditation of my heart be acceptable to you, O Lord, my rock and my redeemer.

❖   ❖   ❖

The ancient Hebrews believed that words once spoken became a measurable thing with weight and volume like a brick or flower. There was no such concept as "taking back something I said" because as soon as the word is spoken they exist in time and place on their own. With the hail of words that come at us from a variety of sources, we would be wise to wear flak jackets. Words do have incredible power and they do linger long after the conversation is done. We are called to be good stewards of our words and thoughts. We can choose to fling brick words back at those who fling them at us, or we can choose to pass them through the filter of God's grace for us.

❖   ❖   ❖

Bless, O Lord, the words that are mine and thine and forgive those that are mine alone. Amen.

AUGUST ◆ 28

I Kings 19:11-12
11He said, "Go out and stand on the mountain before the Lord, for the Lord is about to pass by." Now there was a great wind, so strong that it was splitting mountains and breaking rocks in pieces before the Lord, but the Lord was not in the wind; and after the wind an earthquake, but the Lord was not in the earthquake; 12and after the earthquake a fire, but the Lord was not in the fire; and after the fire a sound of sheer silence.

❖   ❖   ❖

I live in a coastal region that has been heavily damaged in the past by hurricanes. Even still, storms are not given too much attention. A person who recently experienced an earthquake in California simply described it "like someone jiggling the back of your chair." People in the gulf coast region who have experienced the wrath of previous storms don't get too worried about more minor ones. California folks give a casual nod to the earthquake. It makes you wonder what it would really take to get our attention. God chose not to speak to Elijah out of the wind, the earthquake, or the fire but out of the silence. He spoke in a voice that was not an ear-piercing shout. If we are trying to have a conversation with God, the challenge for us all is finding moments of silences and actually listening when we find them.

❖   ❖   ❖

Lord God, may we not be so quick to fill our silence moments with noise so that we may hear your voice. Amen.

August ◆ 29

Psalm 85:7-9
Show us your steadfast love, O Lord, and grant us your salvation. Let me hear what God the Lord will speak, for he will speak peace to his people, to his faithful, to those who turn to him in their hearts. Surely his salvation is at hand for those who fear him, that his glory may dwell in our land.

❖ ❖ ❖

There is an oft-repeated story of a young child who after a nightmare was being comforted by his parent with the words, "God is always with you." The child replied, "I know but sometimes I need something with skin on." As "spiritual" as our culture claims it is, we still need to see, hear, and feel love in tangible ways. Jesus came so that we might have the flesh and blood of a Savior delivering God's love and grace to us. The struggle for us is believing the witness of those who have seen, heard, and touched him. We want to see for ourselves. I believe we will see for ourselves one day. So the question becomes, can we wait and live powerfully faithful lives in the mean time?

❖ ❖ ❖

Holy God, we believe and hope that we can and will see your face, hear your voice and know the power of your salvation. Amen.

August ◆ 30

Psalm 71:20-21
You who have made me see many troubles and calamities will revive me again; from the depths of the earth you will bring me up again. You will increase my honor, and comfort me once again.

❖ ❖ ❖

We can spin our minds into a gelatinous puddle trying to understand the all-knowing, all powerful nature of God. We can walk away from believing in a God who would allow bad things to happen. We can sit in our own private ash heap and ponder our pitiful state. Or we can believe in a God who comes again. My experience has been of a God who trumps every "again" the world or I have thrown at him. When I have been in trouble, God is with me again. When I am in the pits, God again is deeper still to raise me up. When again I feel the pain of living, God again grants me the joy of another day. Even as the struggles come again, I wait with a growing confidence for God's "again."

❖ ❖ ❖

We know you love us and forgive us, Lord. Do it again. Amen.

AUGUST ◆ 31

Matthew 14:22-24
Immediately he made the disciples get into the boat and go on ahead to the other side, while he dismissed the crowds. And after he had dismissed the crowds, he went up the mountain by himself to pray. When evening came, he was there alone, but by this time the boat, battered by the waves, was far from the land, for the wind was against them.

❖ ❖ ❖

The juxtaposition of a lone man praying peacefully on a mountain top next to a group of men being slammed around by wind and waves is too glaring a comparison to ignore. We have more in common with the battered boatload than we do a figure in solitary prayer. And though we recognize it, we still choose the boat in motion over the point of stillness because we have things to do, appointments to keep, people to see, and on and on it goes. The picture Jesus gives us of life with him and without him is dramatically different. And then he bridges the gap between us with himself and invites us into a relationship of faith that changes everything. Every moment. Every thought. Every dream.

❖ ❖ ❖

Holy God, hear our prayer and walk with us so that wherever we are and whatever we are doing will be what makes for peace. Amen.

SEPTEMBER ◆ 1

Isaiah 56:6-7
And the foreigners who join themselves to the Lord, to minister to him, to love the name of the Lord, and to be his servants, all who keep the Sabbath, and do not profane it, and hold fast my covenant- these I will bring to my holy mountain, and make them joyful in my house of prayer; their burnt offerings and their sacrifices will be accepted on my altar; for my house shall be called a house of prayer for all peoples.

❖   ❖   ❖

You know about one of those days. You know what I mean, when routines and disciplines get thrown out of whack by some different event and the day tumbles along and at the end of it, you are just glad that it is the end of it. What separates the foreigner from the native in the scripture lesson is prayer. Days never do follow the pattern that I want them to follow. Things fall through the cracks and it is worse yet, when it is people who fall through the cracks. The difference between the days when I feel at home inside my own skin and the days when I feel like a foreigner to myself is prayer. As soon as we call upon the name of the Lord, God surrounds us with home.

❖   ❖   ❖

Holy God, we enter into this day knowing the minutes of it are gifts, the people in it are treasures, and the love you give us is meant to overflow. Amen.

SEPTEMBER ◆ 2

Psalm 67:1-3
May God be gracious to us and bless us and make his face to shine upon us, that your way may be known upon earth, your saving power among all nations. Let the peoples praise you, O God; let all the peoples praise you.

❖   ❖   ❖

The fundamental problems of our lives have remained the same throughout human history. We do battle with what we don't like about ourselves, our lives and the world around us. We make our own rules and we break them. We struggle with shame and guilt. We wrestle with fear. The ancient redeeming word of God's grace, his unconditional love, continues to be that which makes for life and freedom. Sophistication and the surrounding contemporary world does not keep us from praising God. Letting as many people within earshot know that there is life and hope in God is not a bad thing.

❖   ❖   ❖

Lord God, you are worthy of our praise from the dawn of time to the future beyond our imagination. Amen.

SEPTEMBER ◆ 3

Psalm 4:1
Answer me when I call, O God of my right! You gave me room when I was in distress.

❖ ❖ ❖

One of the important lessons about being a follower of Jesus came from a visiting pastoral counselor at the college I attended. He was only going to be on campus a few days and his daily appointments were heavily booked. A student who wanted to speak with him but could not find a time resorted to a conversation with him on a sidewalk. When the student recounted the conversation to me, she said, "He put his briefcase down and listened to me." That simple gesture of creating a space in his day for her was a grace that overflowed into her life. Whether through text messages, phone calls, emails, blogs or face-to-face, we need someone to listen. The majority of the work I do is making room to listen. I have no simple solutions for the complex problems that happen to us today but I can put my own briefcase down, lay aside my own agenda and make space for another. The God who made room for our prayers invites us to love by listening.

❖ ❖ ❖

Holy God, may we learn how to love by making room. Amen.

SEPTEMBER ◆ 4

Joshua 24:15
Now if you are unwilling to serve the Lord, choose this day whom you will serve, whether the gods your ancestors served in the region beyond the River or the gods of the Amorites in whose land you are living; but as for me and my household, we will serve the Lord.

❖ ❖ ❖

It is one of the great statements of faith in all the scriptures. Joshua called the leaders of the people together and asked for a commitment. He also let them know that service to multiply gods was not an option. It was time to get off the fence. Humans will serve one god or another. We have the ability to choose the God who has our best interest in his heart and mind rather than the gods of empty activity, the gods of the myth of normal, and the gods of false security. Today and every day, we renew our commitment to God who continues to go great lengths for us.

❖ ❖ ❖

Lord God, time and again you have shown us the steadfastness and trustworthiness of your commitment to us. May we be so faithful. Amen.

SEPTEMBER ◆ 5

Isaiah 51:6
Lift up your eyes to the heavens, and look at the earth beneath; for the heavens will vanish like smoke, the earth will wear out like a garment, and those who live on it will die like gnats; but my salvation will be forever, and my deliverance will never be ended.

❖ ❖ ❖

We are becoming more environmentally conscious. We are more aware of how we are using and abusing our natural resources. "Endangered species" is a phrase that we all understand. Try as we might, the oil will not last forever and some species will go extinct. There is a difference between being good stewards, developing renewable resources and imagining that we can preserve everything just the way it is. We are growing in our concern about what kind of planet the next generations will inherit. We can fuel our stewardship with faithfulness in God whose love is the renewable resource.

❖ ❖ ❖

Precious Lord, may we work shoulder to shoulder to tend to your precious earth and be vigilant in our faith in you now and forever. Amen.

SEPTEMBER ◆ 6

Colossians 3:15
And let the peace of Christ rule in your hearts, to which indeed you were called in the one body. And be thankful.

❖   ❖   ❖

We allow ourselves to be influenced in a variety of ways. The marketing industry spends billions of dollars to garner our attention to influence our choices. From junk mail to pop-up ads on the computer to a storm of television images, we stand in a hurricane of messages convincing us to look and choose. God gave us the freedom to choose so that we would enjoy a relationship with him as his children not his puppets. We can allow ourselves to be influenced by those who would buy our attention and obedience. We can just as easily allow ourselves to be ruled by the peace of Christ. This Christ requires nothing more from us than a life of thanksgiving.

❖   ❖   ❖

Now thank we all our God with hearts and hands and voices. Amen.

SEPTEMBER ◆ 7

Romans 12:2
Do not be conformed to this world, but be transformed by the renewing of your minds, so that you may discern what is the will of God-what is good and acceptable and perfect.

❖ ❖ ❖

The trend in jeans never ceases to amaze me. They have gone from straight legs to bell-bottom to straight to tight to flare and then they go retro which is another way of saying they go back and forth again. Everything old is new again. What goes around, comes around. Is there really anything that is genuinely new? I am sure that I have heard this before and said this before. Is there such a thing as a totally original thought? I wish I could be the creator of an original thought, but I would never be sure. I have become convinced, however, that God has an original thought and that thought is me...and it is you. Thanks be to God!

❖ ❖ ❖

Holy God, for your incredible imagination, your original thoughts, your constantly new ways of grace...we give you thanks. Amen.

SEPTEMBER ◆ 8

Matthew 16:19
I will give you the keys of the kingdom of heaven, and whatever you bind on earth will be bound in heaven, and whatever you loose on earth will be loosed in heaven."

❖   ❖   ❖

In a previous congregation I served, we built a new sanctuary and renovated the old one into a fellowship hall. The transition process was a bittersweet one for many who had deep affection for the old space. The new space was dramatically different and felt like a stranger to them. We had a parish member cut small crosses out of the old communion rails and fashioned them into key chains. We made keys to the new sanctuary for every member of the congregation. It was risky, we knew, but it was worth the look on the faces as they received their key. I can't even begin to imagine holding the keys of the kingdom but that is precisely what we have been given. Those keys are confession and forgiveness, mercy and grace. It is how the door was opened for us and now we are empowered with those keys as well.

❖   ❖   ❖

You are awesome, O Lord, in your trust. May we honor your trust with a willing heart for the sake of others. Amen.

SEPTEMBER ◆ 9

Psalm 34: 17-20
The righteous cry, and the Lord hears them and delivers them from all their troubles. The Lord is near to the brokenhearted and will save whose spirits are crushed. Many are the troubles of the righteous, but the Lord will deliver him out of them all. He will keep safe all his bones; not one of them shall be broken.

❖ ❖ ❖

One of the characteristics of the righteous that we often overlook is that the righteous ones don't know who they are. It is not a title we can claim for ourselves, but one which is given to us by God. Everyone cries. Everyone has troubles. God cares about the ones he has claimed as his own and God cares about the ones who are at the end of their rope. No matter the sender - when the cry is sent in God's direction - God hears and God cares.

❖ ❖ ❖

Holy God, hear our prayer and may our lives reflect your gracious love. Amen.

SEPTEMBER ◆ 10

Jeremiah 15:16
Your words were found, and I ate them, and your words became to me a joy and the delight of my heart; for I am called by your name, O Lord, God of hosts.

❖ ❖ ❖

"Eating words" is usually a phrase for taking back a comment we made. In scripture, the eating of words is symbol for learning, gaining wisdom and integrating knowledge into our lives. In John's Gospel Jesus becomes "The Word." Jesus offers himself as body and blood in and through the bread and wine to take in God's Word so that we allow Christ to change us from the inside out. As advanced as our technology has become and will become, words will never lose their power and importance. We are what we eat.

❖ ❖ ❖

Holy God, may we be nurtured by your life-giving word. Amen.

SEPTEMBER ◆ 11

Psalm 26:11-12a
But as for me, I walk in my integrity; redeem me, and be gracious to me. My foot stands on level ground.

❖   ❖   ❖

When I went to New Zealand to hike the Milford Track, I thought I knew what I was getting into but no one is fully prepared for such an extraordinary experience. I did not expect to be so blown away by the beauty. I did not expect to need so profoundly the help of those who walked with me. I did not expect that walking down was just as difficult as walking up because the path was uneven and rocky. My walking poles were an absolute necessity. They eased the strain my knees with every step. To walk in our integrity is to live in the truth about ourselves. We are sinners in need of redeeming, saints who have been given grace upon grace. The truth is that we cannot make this journey without help.

❖   ❖   ❖

Precious Lord, take my hand, lead me on, let me stand. Amen.

SEPTEMBER ◆ 12

Romans 12:9-11
Let love be genuine; hate what is evil, hold fast to what is good; love one another with mutual affection; outdo one another in showing honor. Do not lag in zeal, be ardent in spirit, serve the Lord.

❖ ❖ ❖

I have had jet lag from time to time. I had moments that I barely recognized myself in the mirror. It took me to respond to someone's question. I have lagged in zeal more often than I want to admit. At our weekly chapel service for our Early Learning Center, dozens of pre-school children who do not want to hear about jet lag or zeal lag. They don't want to hear that I have a lot on my mind or everything I have to do that day or that I want another cup of coffee NOW! The children are there to worship God in their way and they need my zeal not to lag. Somehow, it is always easy to get jazzed for them. When we are called outside of ourselves for others, the spirit of the Living Christ jazzes us.

❖ ❖ ❖

Lord God, stir our faith and hearts that we might have the energy and the will to love with mad abandon. Amen.

SEPTEMBER ◆ 13

Jeremiah 33:16
In those days Judah will be saved and Jerusalem will live in safety. And this is the name by which it will be called: "The Lord is our righteousness."

❖ ❖ ❖

In order to reach a new generation, we are having to look carefully at the "church" words that we throw around expecting that everyone understands what they mean. Righteousness is one of those words that makes people glaze over because it isn't a word that is a part of their daily discourse. Chances are righteousness is never a part of a text message. We know that a self-righteous person is not anyone we want to be or be around. We throw out the baby with the bath water by letting go of the word righteousness all together. It is a state of being that we all desperately need. We need to know that we are exactly where we need to be and exactly who we need to be in relationship to ourselves, our world and our God. We can't declare that for ourselves without sounding arrogant and ignoring God. God offers himself to us so that, in him, we are made right. We may not fling the word righteousness around on a daily basis, but it is in knowing that we are completely made right in God that helps us fall asleep at night.

❖ ❖ ❖

Lord God, help us to stand in the right place at the right time for the right reason and enjoy the moment. Amen.

SEPTEMBER ◆ 14

Deuteronomy 30:19-20
I call heaven and earth to witness against you today that I have set before you, life and death, blessings and curses. Choose life so that you and your descendants may live, loving the Lord your God, obeying him, and holding fast to him; for that means life to you and length of days, so that you may live in the land that the Lord swore to give to your ancestors, to Abraham, to Isaac, and to Jacob.

❖   ❖   ❖

In the movie "The Matrix," the main hero, Neo is faced with a choices – the red pill or the blue pill. One way may lead to a good life, but it means living a lie. Another way is the truth, but filled with difficulty and pain. The overriding theme of the movie is being free to make one's own choices. God does not want to create a fantasy world in which we believe that we have choices when we do not. God, in fact, gives us real choices that present the possibility of not choosing God. We have the freedom to choose those things, attitudes and actions that are life affirming and those things which are not. Let us decide today to be God's people in this day, honoring his commandments and loving God's people. Let us choose life.

❖   ❖   ❖

Holy God, the choices you have given us are an awesome privilege. Help us to see clearly the choice of loving you who loves us so well. Amen.

SEPTEMBER ◆ 15

Psalm 1:1
Happy are those who do not follow the advice of the wicked, or take the path that sinners tread, or sit in the seat of scoffers.

❖   ❖   ❖

Once I played the game of "Follow the Leader" as a child with a few friends I had not known very long. I was anxious to fit in and belong. At one point during the game the leader walked through a drain pipe that ran underneath a road. The space was passable but small, damp, moldy and filled with all manner of slithering and crawling things. I didn't follow. I got teased for my cowardice. I found new friends. Sometimes the decisions we have to make are not that clean cut, but even in our adulthood we continue to follow, to want to fit in. We are willing to risk a great deal for that comfort. God gives us the comfort of belonging always and completely in his care.

❖   ❖   ❖

Holy God, help us to recognize the paths before us and to choose wisely and well where we belong.

SEPTEMBER ◆ 16

Philemon 1:3-4
Grace to you and peace from God our Father and the Lord Jesus Christ. When I remember you in my prayers, I always thank my God because I hear of your love for all the saints and your faith toward the Lord Jesus.

❖ ❖ ❖

I have used a variation of Paul's greeting to start all of my sermons since the beginning of my career. Even as the years have passed those words remind me of the ancient legacy of the proclamation of the Gospel which vibrated through the centuries. The sound of grace and the love of God has survived the rise and fall of countries, the changes in cultures and the apathy of Christians. We are called to greet one another with encouragement and prayers. Through the sound of those greetings we contribute to the history of the Gospel ringing well and true in every generation.

❖ ❖ ❖

Holy God, you bless us with the ancient echoes of faithful heroes. Help us to carry the sound of grace into our world. Amen.

SEPTEMBER ◆ 17

Luke 14:28-30
For which of you, intending to build a tower, does not first sit down and estimate the cost, to see whether he has enough to complete it? Otherwise, when he has laid a foundation and is not able to finish, all who see it will begin to ridicule him, saying, 'This fellow began to build and was not able to finish.'

❖ ❖ ❖

Jesus turns to a crowd following him. There is a difference between disciples of Jesus Christ and curious on-lookers. Jesus tells them not to start what they can't finish, to count the cost before they begin. We live in such a consumer-driven, throw-away culture that we expect that if one model or brand of something fails us we will try another. What we value in our lives seems to shift with the days as well. What Jesus requires of us is probably even more difficult for our generation - he requires our complete attention. Discipleship in Jesus Christ is a way of life not just a passing thought.

❖ ❖ ❖

Lord God, what you ask of us is so huge but what you have to offer is more than we can imagine. Take us and use us as you will. Amen.

SEPTEMBER ◆ 18

Exodus 32:13-14
Remember Abraham, Isaac, and Israel, your servants, how you swore to them by your own self, saying to them, 'I will multiply your descendants like the stars of heaven, and all this land that I have promised I will give to your descendants, and they shall inherit it forever.'" And the Lord changed his mind about the disaster that he planned to bring on his people.

❖   ❖   ❖

I heard about a mother suspected of intentionally overdosing her drug-addicted daughter to claim the daughter's infant son as her own and collect the life insurance. For most of us, that level of human depravity is at a distance in news stories or in television drama plots. When Moses left his people to go up the mountain to listen to God, the people quickly disintegrated into a fearful rabble with misguided leadership. God got angry. God thought about wiping them all out and starting over again but he didn't. He kept his promises even to a people who were criminally self-absorbed. As much as possible, we are to be merchants of hope for people who may be on the brink of losing their humanity. We have hope to offer in the one who has kept his promises to us.

❖   ❖   ❖

Holy God, kindle the fires of hope in us so that we might be a light for those wandering in the darkness. Amen.

SEPTEMBER ◆ 19

Numbers 11:17
I will come down and talk with you there; and I will take some of the spirit that is on you and put it on them; and they shall bear the burden of the people along with you so that you will not bear it all by yourself.

❖ ❖ ❖

If I have learned anything in life and in my work in the Christian community, it is that the burdens do not go away. We may be able temporarily to move our intense worries and concerns to the side, but they are waiting and urgent. We lift them like children who have grown too heavy for their mother's hip and they insist on being carried. I have watched parents pass their children around at family gatherings. It is not lack of love but the necessity of sharing the burden of the never-ending responsibility of caring for our little ones. No one was meant to carry burdens alone. God chose to allow leadership to be shared. Jesus chose to work with 12 disciples and give them authority. Even as we criticize our leaders, we are well to remember that the responsibility of the work God has given us to do is a shared one. We honor God when we do our part in bearing the burdens and when we allow others to help us bear ours.

❖ ❖ ❖

Holy God, may we shoulder the loads motivated by the love for others. Amen.

SEPTEMBER ◆ 20

James 5:16
Therefore confess your sins to one another, and pray for one another, so that you may be healed. The prayer of the righteous is powerful and effective.

❖ ❖ ❖

When it comes to conflict with one another we run in extremes. We never admit we are wrong or we hand out cheap "I'm sorry" like a Pez dispenser. We manage conflict instead of ministering to it. The tools God has given us for conflict with one another is for healing and restoration, not control. In our urgency, control often seems like a better goal and so we don't use the tools we are given. The tools are confession, forgiveness and prayer. Confession is admitting we are wrong. Forgiveness is saying that our relationship matters more than the hurt we have experienced. Prayer puts us all in the hands of the one who can make right what we make wrong, heal our brokenness and quiet our anger. God has given us tools because He already knows we will need them. Any good worker knows, it is all in the right tools. And so it is.

❖ ❖ ❖

Holy God, thank you for the Spirit's work to move us toward one another in spite of our differences. Amen.

SEPTEMBER ◆ 21

Luke 15:18
I will get up and go to my father, and I will say to him, "Father, I have sinned against heaven and before you; I am no longer worthy to be called your son; treat me like one of your hired hands."' So he set off and went to his father. But while he was still far off, his father saw him and was filled with compassion; he ran and put his arms around him and kissed him.

❖ ❖ ❖

I love that line...."while he was still far off, his father saw him." The father must have been looking. I lost a dog once and I never stopped looking for her even years later when I knew that she had long since died. There was something in me that just kept looking. I lost a student once to death, but I saw him everywhere years later in crowds and passing on sidewalks. There was something in me that kept looking. We are created in the image of God - we are wired for hope even in the face of hopelessness. During the times when we feel the most lost ourselves and far off, it is good to remember that our God will keep looking and never give up hope.

❖ ❖ ❖

Precious Lord, for your relentless compassion we give you thanks. Amen.

SEPTEMBER ◆ 22

Psalm 71:18-19
So even to old age and gray hairs, O God, do not forsake me, until I proclaim your might to all the generations to come. Your power and your righteousness, O God, reach the high heavens. You who have done great things, O God, who is like you?

❖   ❖   ❖

There is a list published every year by a university which gives a snapshot of the mindset of incoming college freshmen. One year's list indicated that these 18 year olds have likely never worn a wristwatch. They think email is too slow. To them, Clint Eastwood is a movie director, Beethoven is a dog and Michelangelo was a computer virus. The list always makes me feel like I have personally beaten the color out of every strand of my hair. The gap widens between the generations all the time. What we have in common is that every generation still needs what God has to offer. Our need for unconditional love, real forgiveness and a sense of belonging never leaves us, no matter if there is a spring in our step or a winter in our bones. God is great. Tell everyone.

❖   ❖   ❖

Holy God, may every generation see and believe your steadfast love. Amen.

SEPTEMBER ◆ 23

Amos 8:11-12
The time is surely coming, says the Lord God, when I will send a famine on the land; not a famine of bread, or a thirst for water, but of hearing the words of the Lord. They shall wander from sea to sea, and from north to east; they shall run to and fro, seeking the word of the Lord, but they shall not find it.*

❖   ❖   ❖

Of the punishments of childhood, none were greater than the times when my father would stop talking. As an adult, I still squirm like a child when my friends fall silent. We have all known the hunger for a word from someone important to us. In the history of the people of God, sometimes the disciplining method was a famine of words. In the loneliness, the people of God learned anew the priority of God's presence in their lives. I am not sure that we are as astute to recognize our divine hunger for God's word these days. It may come to us in the night when we hit our pillows and can't make sense of the day. It may come to us in the melancholy that drifts around us as we drive to work. Whatever way we experience the hollowness, we are being called by the God who loves us to hunger for his company.

❖   ❖   ❖

Lord God, we yearn for your presence, your wisdom, your grace. Help us to listen. Amen.

SEPTEMBER ◆ 24

Psalm 113:1-3
Praise the Lord! Praise, O servants of the Lord; praise the name of the Lord. Blessed be the name of the Lord from this time on and forevermore. From the rising of the sun to its setting the name of the Lord is to be praised.

❖ ❖ ❖

No matter our best efforts as we move into a new day, it is easy to get sucked into the vortex of the petty issues that seem to swirl around clusters of humanity like dust balls that flee from the sweep of a broom. My days begin well when I remember that this is truly God's day and I have the privilege of being in it. My days end well when I remember the grace that allows me to sleep. The part that gives me headaches are all the minutes in between our waking and our sleeping when we forget anything about God and stomp around as if sinning was our human right rather than the worst of our nature. Someone once said that character is who we are when only God is watching. Perhaps our best character is revealed when we praise God all day and that we praise him best by remembering who we are in him from sunrise to sunset.

❖ ❖ ❖

Holy God, we praise you with our thoughts, words and deeds. Amen.

SEPTEMBER ◆ 25

I Timothy 2:,8
First of all, then, I urge that supplications, prayers, intercessions, and thanksgivings be made for everyone. I desire, then, that in every place the men should pray, lifting up holy hands without anger or argument.

❖ ❖ ❖

Teachers, camp counselors, leaders of all sorts have some method of getting people's attention when they need to quiet the crowd and get them to focus away from private conversations to the matter at hand. Some whistle, some wave their hands, some shout "Attention, everyone!" After several years in campus ministry with the Aggies of Texas A&M University, I learned that "Howdy!" was very effective. In the church community, nothing works as effectively as "Let us pray!" Even and especially in the Christian family, a group can become a restless and angry mob. To pray is to enter the quiet of a cathedral no matter where we are and no matter who we are fighting with or about. When we find ourselves angry with someone, to pray for them creates a space for grace in which God can quiet our thoughts and help us to respond with wisdom and mercy.

❖ ❖ ❖

Holy God, help us to heed your call to constant prayer so that we may live and serve constantly in your presence and wisdom. Amen.

SEPTEMBER ◆ 26

Luke 16:10-13
"Whoever is faithful in a very little is faithful also in much; and whoever is dishonest in a very little is dishonest also in much. If then you have not been faithful with the dishonest wealth, who will entrust to you the true riches? And if you have not been faithful with what belongs to another, who will give you what is your own? No slave can serve two masters; for a slave will either hate the one and love the other, or be devoted to the one and despise the other. You cannot serve God and wealth."

❖ ❖ ❖

I met a teenage boy who was quite the entrepreneur! He bought candy in quantity at a discount store and sold it for a profit at school. He was learning great lessons in supply and demand and profit margin. I applauded him on his efforts. I seized the opportunity for a teaching moment about charitable giving and tithing. When he did the math and figured out that ten percent of his profits sounded so little it was easy for him to say, "Sure! I can do that!" Later in life when we become adults, 10 percent of our salaries sounds too much for our budgets to handle. It is certainly easier to start tithing when we are young, when the amount isn't so overwhelming. God rejoices in our offerings no matter the size. Few of us tithe but it doesn't mean that we can't grow in that direction.

❖ ❖ ❖

Holy God, help us to grow in our giving and to be faithful in all that you have given us. Amen.

SEPTEMBER ◆ 27

John 12:30
Jesus answered, "This voice has come for your sake, not for mine."

❖   ❖   ❖

People who have children say that their priorities change. Parents think of themselves less and focus necessarily on the needs of their children. Children need someone to help them learn, deal with their feelings, get along with others, and explore their gifts. Most especially, they need love in the form of grace and forgiveness so that they can have security in their role in the family and peace inside their own skin. The problem is that people who have children don't stop needing the same things that all children need. Sometimes we adults look around and there is no one to forgive us and assure us that we still belong. We have moments of selflessness for the sake of others, especially our children. The rest of the time we are truly lost. Jesus emptied himself for us that everyone could find their way home. We never stop being God's first priority.

❖   ❖   ❖

Lord, grant us the freedom of your grace to love others as we have been loved. Amen.

SEPTEMBER ◆ 28

Mark 9:32
But they did not understand what he was saying and were afraid to ask him.

❖ ❖ ❖

There are days when I envy the experience of the disciples sitting at the Lord's feet. I try to imagine myself sitting by a fire in the night, riveted to Jesus' face and voice, aware of the other faces around me not unlike my own and wanting the moment to last forever. It doesn't take too many years of living to know that all things end, magical moments melt away and slip through the sieve of time. Even more painfully, relationships end and hearts are broken. All we can do is hang on for as long as we can, live in the memory or in denial. Jesus tells his disciples he will be killed and after his death, he will rise again. In the minds of the disciples those words must have frozen and confused them. All that the Lord had said up to that moment they hoped in their heart would be true. They sat on the other side of Easter, suddenly lonely and afraid. The part about rising from the dead was too much to hope for but too good not to.

❖ ❖ ❖

Lord, we cling to you and your words of hope and promise and believe in you. Amen.

SEPTEMBER ◆ 29

I Timothy 6:12
Fight the good fight of the faith; take hold of the eternal life, to which you were called and for which you made the good confession in the presence of many witnesses.

❖ ❖ ❖

There are days when everything feels like a struggle. Getting out of bed is a struggle. Getting kids ready for school is a struggle. Communicating with our friends, family, co-workers is a struggle. Getting through traffic is a struggle. Finding time to do everything necessary is a struggle. We only have so much energy, so much time in a day and sometimes it is a struggle to know which struggle is worth the struggle. On my office wall is a sword and shield, it reminds me every day of the armor of God - the shield of faith and the sword of the Word of God. It also reminds me to fight the good fight...to be engaged in the struggle for the sake of God's mission in the world and not just my own "to do" list. That we face our daily struggles is a given....what God is calling us to do is pick our battles wisely for the kingdom's sake.

❖ ❖ ❖

Almighty God, help us this day to fight the good fight. Amen.

SEPTEMBER ◆ 30

James 3:13
Who is wise and understanding among you? Show by your good life that your works are done with gentleness born of wisdom.

❖   ❖   ❖

Some of the people who have made the largest impact in my life have not been the noisy ones or those prone to heights and depths of emotion, but rather the ones who gently move thoughtfully and deliberately through their days. We want to extend a hand to touch them as if to believe their gentleness might be viral and infect us with peace. Robert Frost wrote in a poem "So when at times the mob is swayed to carry praise or blame to far - we may choose something like a star to stay our minds on and be stayed." When we find peace in the firm and gentle grip of a scarred but living hand, we are set free to work and to will God's grace through the living of our days.

❖   ❖   ❖

Precious Lord, steady my nerves, assure me of your grace and set me solidly on your way. Amen.

OCTOBER ◆ 1

Mark 9:42
If any of you put a stumbling block before one of these little ones who believe in me...

❖   ❖   ❖

Driven by a sweet tooth, I managed to break the commandment about not stealing at an early age. I would steal candy bars from a local market near my school. My career as a thief didn't last much more than a week, but long enough to have taught a classmate my criminal techniques. I felt guilty enough for the crime, but as the years went along I felt even more guilty about enticing someone else to sin. I have known my share of stumbling blocks in my journey of faith. I learned early, however, that I could BE a stumbling block as easily as I could have one. One of the great wonders of God's economy is that the more we resist hurting others, the more strength we will have to overcome the obstacles thrown our way. If we concentrate only on walking the straight and narrow ourselves, we may miss the opportunity to help someone over their difficulties. To lose ourselves in order to find ourselves may not make much sense but it is a powerful way to love.

❖   ❖   ❖

Lord God, forgive our self-absorbed focus and help us find ourselves in loving others. Amen.

OCTOBER ◆ 2

Ezekiel 33:7
So you, mortal, I have made a sentinel for the house of Israel; whenever you hear a word from my mouth, you shall give them warning from me.

❖ ❖ ❖

Now living in an area which is vulnerable to hurricanes, I have learned what it takes to prepare for storm. Property insurance is costly. Supplies are needed to store. Preparations need to be made for power failures. Weather warnings are heeded with heightened interest. Evacuation routes and timing are crucial decisions. Of course, not every storm warrants all of the preparations, but not to pay attention would be foolish. Those who have heard many warnings in the course of their life weary of the preparations and may ignore the warnings. I deeply appreciate the work that the scientists do who study the weather so that we can be warned. Even more so, we appreciate the God who guides, corrects and loves his people enough to discipline them to listen so that we will hear the warning as love.

Holy God, speak to us in ways that we will hear and understand what you are calling us to do and be. Amen.

OCTOBER ◆ 3

Romans 13:11-12
Besides this, you know what time it is, how it is now the moment for you to wake from sleep. For salvation is nearer to us now than when we became believers; the night is far gone, the day is near. Let us then lay aside the works of darkness and put on the armor of light

❖ ❖ ❖

Author C.S. Lewis described our lives now as if we were walking the alley ways of a city where the only source of light was coming from a brightly lit city square. Some of the light spills into the alleys, but we walk still in the shadowlands. When we were children, we were afraid of the dark, in our adulthood we are afraid of the light. Jesus pierced the darkness with his own body. If we listen carefully from the shadowlands where we are standing, we can hear him in the city square calling, "Ally, Ally, in free."

❖ ❖ ❖

Holy God, we have learned to hide from the light instead of seeking it out. Help us to move out of the darkness into your light. Amen.

OCTOBER ◆ 4

Jeremiah 4:26-7
I looked, and lo, the fruitful land was a desert, and all its cities were laid in ruins before the Lord, before his fierce anger. For thus says the Lord: The whole land shall be a desolation; yet I will not make a full end.

❖ ❖ ❖

A bishop I once knew years ago would often preach in a variety of churches and yet, often, based his sermons on texts from Jeremiah. Like Jeremiah, the bishop's job included having to deliver an honest but tough message to a church family. The people were messing up both individually and collectively and there were consequences for their bad behavior and hard hearts. God was angry and disappointed. Jeremiah's message was the stuff no one wants to hear. The consequences were severe. I can understand the anger, the disappointed, and the severe consequences. Who among us is so perfect that we do not understand the need for chastisement, course correction and punishment for the sake of changing death-dealing behavior? Before we fling stones at the messenger or turn or cold shoulder to God we might do well to stare at the word 'desolation' as what we deserve, but notice that the sentence doesn't end with judgment. There is the seed of grace and mercy inside the word "yet." With that, we can take that "yet" and enter into a new day, a new relationship, a new hope.

❖ ❖ ❖

Thank you, Lord, for not letting what we deserve to be the last word in our relationship. Amen.

OCTOBER ◆ 5

Genesis 50:15-18
Realizing that their father was dead, Joseph's brothers said, "What if Joseph still bears a grudge against us and pays us back in full for all the wrong that we did to him?" So they approached Joseph, saying, "Your father gave this instruction before he died, 'Say to Joseph: I beg you, forgive the crime of your brothers and the wrong they did in harming you.' Now therefore please forgive the crime of the servants of the God of your father." Joseph wept when they spoke to him. Then his brothers also wept, fell down before him, and said, "We are here as your slaves."

❖ ❖ ❖

The brothers' scheme to save their sorry lives worked. They got what they didn't deserve - Joseph's mercy and forgiveness. The brothers who removed Joseph from his family, sold him to traders, convinced his father he was dead, now are willing to be Joseph's slaves to save themselves from Joseph's justifiable revenge and the regional famine. The end doesn't always justify the means but the end was reconciliation. We have all known a pretty bumpy journey in our lives of faith. It isn't pretty and our motives are never always pure and yet, God receives us, forgives us and loves us beyond our imagination. I would rather be a slave to God than a champion of my own foolishness.

❖ ❖ ❖

Holy God, forgive our selfish schemes and bless the confessions of a contrite heart. Amen.

OCTOBER ◆ 6

Psalm 125
Those who trust in the Lord are like Mount Zion, which cannot be moved, but abides forever. As the mountains surround Jerusalem, so the Lord surrounds his people, from this time on and forevermore.

❖   ❖   ❖

A native of North Dakota once told me that there was a sign as one crossed the state line into his state that proudly declared, "Welcome to North Dakota! Home of the most successful mountain removal project in history." We like to think we can move mountains but more often than not, we are the mountain of stubbornness or wrong thinking or criticism that needs to be moved. God's forgiveness and relentless grace can move such a mountain. For those of you who get to see actual mountains on a daily basis, may they remind you of the God who surrounds and protects you. For those of us who live in places that look more like North Dakota, God is the only mountain we will ever know but that's okay.

❖   ❖   ❖

God, protect us and strengthen us so that we might be a witness to your love and grace. Amen.

OCTOBER ◆ 7

Romans 14:7-12
We do not live to ourselves, and we do not die to ourselves. If we live, we live to the Lord, and if we die, we die to the Lord; so then, whether we live or whether we die, we are the Lord's. For to this end Christ died and lived again, so that he might be Lord of both the dead and the living. Why do you pass judgment on your brother or sister? Or you, why do you despise your brother or sister? For we will all stand before the judgment seat of God. For it is written, "As I live, says the Lord, every knee shall bow to me, and every tongue shall give praise to God." So then, each of us will be accountable to God.

❖   ❖   ❖

In the Star Trek television series, the worst enemy that the Enterprise crew ever encountered was "The Borg." It was an alien life form that sought to assimilate everything and everyone into its collective mind and obliterate individuality. Even in the minds of science fiction writers, the treasure of our own will is prized above all. We need to be careful what we wish for. We want our individuality to be honored, but who will honor it if we shove one another away from us? Together and individually, we belong to God who is able to love and cherish each person and yet call us to accountability to one another. It is a pretty good deal if we think about it.

❖   ❖   ❖

Holy God, we give you thanks for the freedom to be ourselves and the joy of being your children. Amen.

OCTOBER ◆ 8

Habbakuk 2:1-4
I will stand at my watch post, and station myself on the rampart; I will keep watch to see what he will say to me, and what he will answer concerning my complaint. Then the Lord answered me and said: Write the vision; make it plain on tablets, so that a runner may read it. For there is still a vision for the appointed time; it speaks of the end, and does not lie. If it seems to tarry, wait for it; it will surely come, it will not delay. Look at the proud! Their spirit is not right in them, but the righteous live by their faith.

❖ ❖ ❖

From what I have witnessed, marathon runners and cancer patients have an important common experience. Even though they run their respective races alone, they have a support team who wave signs in various ways for encouragement. If we are to catch God's vision for us and keep it before us on a daily basis we need it clearly stated on a big sign that can be easily read by someone running an important race. When the circumstances of life wipe away our energy and our hope, we have to dig deeper still. When we do, it is important that we can see Jesus. It is important that people can see Jesus in us.

❖ ❖ ❖

Holy God, give us a vision that we might run the race set before us today with confidence and peace. Amen.

OCTOBER ◆ 9

Psalm 37
Be still before the Lord, and wait patiently for him; do not fret over those who prosper in their way, over those who carry out evil devices. Refrain from anger, and forsake wrath. Do not fret-it leads only to evil.

❖   ❖   ❖

When I take a trip which usually involves sitting, it never ceases to amaze me how much it can wear me out. Even when I am the passenger, I get weary and when the car stops there is a deep sense of relief. It is not unlike that blessed moment when I settle into bed for the night. Stillness is a rare event for most people yet it is the place to which God calls us to wait for him. God chases us through our days and meets us especially when we stop to breath. What we breathe in is God's spirit of life. We are just asked not to waste that new breath being angry.

❖   ❖   ❖

Holy God, chase us, find us, still us and help us breathe. Amen.

OCTOBER ◆ 10

I Timothy 1:6
For this reason I remind you to rekindle the gift of God that is within you through the laying on of my hands; for God did not give us a spirit of cowardice, but rather a spirit of power and of love and of self-discipline.

❖   ❖   ❖

Anyone that has ever been camping knows that fires need to be tended. Of course, it needs to be kept in control to protect the forest. But to do what it was intended to do means a camp fire has to be focused and fed. So also with the gifts that we have been given by God. We have plenty coming at us on a daily basis to distract or to douse the flame. The fire itself is not of our own making, but it is our task to keep it kindled by being the people God created us to be. Focused gifts of God are powerful vehicles for love.

❖   ❖   ❖

Lord God, light the fire within us so that we might be bold in our love for ourselves, others and the world. Amen.

OCTOBER ◆ 11

Luke 17:5-6
The apostles said to the Lord, "Increase our faith!" The Lord replied, "If you had faith the size of a mustard seed, you could say to this mulberry tree, 'Be uprooted and planted in the sea,' and it would obey you.

❖   ❖   ❖

The disciples spoke of faith in quantitative terms and Jesus used a different measurement. The power of faith is not a matter of size but in that it is used. Chances are, if we were capable of enormous power, we would not use it to landscape the ocean. Through the grace of God in Jesus Christ, the fact of the matter is that we do have enormous power. We can use it to change despair into hope, loneliness into community, a heavy burden into a light one. Faith is the muscle we didn't know we had until we use it to shoulder the burden of another child of God.

❖   ❖   ❖

Holy God, make us keenly aware of the faith that we have been given so that we might serve you with power and love. Amen.

OCTOBER ◆ 12

Mark 10:16
And he took them up in his arms, laid his hands on them, and blessed them.

❖   ❖   ❖

"Door Duty" for a pastor is that time-honored ritual of greeting Sunday worshippers at the church door. These little bits of drive-by conversation, momentary eye contact and quick handshakes I've come to value as a method to see how folks are doing. People are creatures of habit and when the greeting changes, it is a signal of something going on & good or bad. There are a few of the children who open their arms as wide as they can to accommodate all my liturgical robes to give me a hug. There is a blessing that finds its way into both of our souls. I cherish the children's trust and I covet every moment I have to let them know that their pastor loves them. In a time when trust is a rare thing and sinfulness makes us necessarily cautious and protective, children still teach us the way to embrace God's kingdom is with open and unfearful arms. The blessing of God certainly happens when we get within arms' reach. Those arms are scarred but full of love.

❖   ❖   ❖

Holy God, help us to draw close to you as you draw close to us. Amen.

OCTOBER ♦ 13

2 Kings 5:9-13
So Naaman came with his horses and chariots, and halted at the entrance of Elisha's house. Elisha sent a messenger to him, saying, "Go, wash in the Jordan seven times, and your flesh shall be restored and you shall be clean." But Naaman became angry and went away, saying, "I thought that for me he would surely come out, and stand and call on the name of the Lord his God, and would wave his hand over the spot, and cure the leprosy! Are not Abana and Pharpar, the rivers of Damascus, better than all the waters of Israel? Could I not wash in them, and be clean?" He turned and went away in a rage. But his servants approached and said to him, "Father, if the prophet had commanded you to do something difficult, would you not have done it? How much more, when all he said to you was, 'Wash, and be clean'?"

❖   ❖   ❖

Naaman was a great warrior who was laid low with a hideous disease and offered a cure. The cure involved getting in his chariot and going to Elisha, the one who could help him. The great warrior bristle that Elisha wouldn't come to him. When the prophet sent out a servant to relay simple instructions, the great warrior stomped away in a huff because the prophet wouldn't meet with him personally. His cure was a few yards away, but his pride made it too far to go. Sometimes, that is all that is standing in the way of what we truly need.

❖   ❖   ❖

Lord God, when we are laid low help us not to let our pride get in the way of your mercy. Amen.

OCTOBER ◆ 14

Psalm 111:7-10
The works of his hands are faithful and just; all his precepts are trustworthy. They are established forever and ever, to be performed with faithfulness and uprightness. He sent redemption to his people; he has commanded his covenant forever. Holy and awesome is his name. The fear of the Lord is the beginning of wisdom; all those who practice it have a good understanding. His praise endures forever.

❖   ❖   ❖

We are a generation which understands the word "recall." Products are recalled by the manufacturer when a flaw is discovered. It is especially news worthy if the flaw would endanger the public. We have quality control experts and government inspections, but mistakes still happen and rules are sometimes bent or broken. Our laws have loopholes that constantly need to be examined and adjusted, but they are never iron-clad. The psalmist tells us that the work of God's hand and his laws are just and trustworthy. We need something in which we can believe will deliver what it promises. God is worthy of our praise.

❖   ❖   ❖

Holy God, you are trustworthy in your laws. Help us to believe and obey. Amen.

OCTOBER ◆ 15

2 Timothy 2:14-15
Remind them of this, and warn them before God that they are to avoid wrangling over words, which does no good but only ruins those who are listening. Do your best to present yourself to God as one approved by him, a worker who has no need to be ashamed, rightly explaining the word of truth.

❖ ❖ ❖

The technological advances this generation has witnessed can make my head spin, but words are still a staple in how we communicate. Words are text messaged, facebooked, and podcasted. The methods change but what we communicate can still be distorted or fabricated. We cannot always believe what we hear or read is the truth. More often than not, it may contain some truth but rarely all of it. As we grow in our understanding of God, we learn to live constantly in his presence. In the presence of the one who loves and forgives us, we need not fear the truth about ourselves and can speak the truth about God as we encounter him in Jesus Christ.

❖ ❖ ❖

Lord God of truth, be the guardian of our mouths and the gatekeeper of our words so that we may speak with love and truth. Amen.

OCTOBER ◆ 16

Luke 17:17-19
Then Jesus asked, "Were not ten made clean? But the other nine, where are they? Was none of them found to return and give praise to God except this foreigner?" Then he said to him, "Get up and go on your way; your faith has made you well."

❖ ❖ ❖

Ten were healed and one returned to give thanks and praise. Living a life of thanksgiving completes the circuit of God's creativity and power. It surges through us for others and God is given the praise. Living a life of thanksgiving is not really a lot to ask given what we have received. Walking through our days as grateful people makes a difference in how we view other people and how we handle the difficulties that come our way. The one who knows that life is a gift is intimately connected forever with the giver.

❖ ❖ ❖

Giver of Life, we praise your name and thank you for your love and grace. Amen.

OCTOBER ◆ 17

Colossians 1:9-10
For this reason, since the day we heard it, we have not ceased praying for you and asking that you may be filled with the knowledge of God's will in all spiritual wisdom and understanding, so that you may lead lives worthy of the Lord, fully pleasing to him, as you bear fruit in every good work and as you grow in the knowledge of God.

❖   ❖   ❖

When we face decisions, we say we want to know God's will. We want to know that we are choosing that path that God will bless and not thwart. We want to feel good about the choice and not be drowning in regret. Even if the path is difficult, we can find comfort in believing that we are doing God's will. Half of the time, if not all of the time, it is less about knowing and doing God's will and more about being at peace inside our own decisions. To grow in the knowledge of God is to know a God who chases us around through all our choices. We reap what we sow. God blesses what God wills. God may or may not bless our decisions. We may or may not know what choice is more God's will than another. When we find ourselves trying to figure out God's will, it is good to remember that WE are God's will. Chances are, if we begin to understand the depth and breadth of God's love, the choices we make will be laced with God's grace.

❖   ❖   ❖

Holy God, may our lives bear the fruit of knowing you. Amen.

OCTOBER ◆ 18

Colossian 1:28-29
It is he whom we proclaim, warning everyone and teaching everyone in all wisdom, so that we may present everyone mature in Christ. For this I toil and struggle with all the energy that he powerfully inspires within me.

❖ ❖ ❖

Somewhere along the way, we turned following Jesus into a disembodied system of occasional thoughts, wishful thinking and intermittent good deeds. Frankly, we have turned following any one person with life-long commitment into a suspicious behavior. We have defined maturity as independence and self-sufficiency. The decision to shape one's life and purpose for living completely and utterly on another person is certainly worthy of our scrutiny. The apostle Paul and the Gospel writers invite us to scrutinize Jesus. Through the scriptures we encounter him as the disciples encountered him. We listen and learn and we make a choice as ancient as the first disciples. Do we follow this Jesus? Maturity in Christ is learning how dependent we are on him for the grace to breath each day. Choosing to follow him each day is likely the wildest and the most mature choice we will ever make.

❖ ❖ ❖

Day by day, Lord, we follow you. Amen.

OCTOBER ◆ 19

Psalm 121:1-2
I lift up my eyes to the hills- from where will my help come?
My help comes from the Lord, who made heaven and earth.

❖ ❖ ❖

In the theater classes I took in college I learned that one of the habits of "rookie" actors is that, in the interest of projecting their voice and trying to remember their lines, they speak them in the direction of the lights on the ceiling. Learning to focus the voice to the audience but remain present with the other actors in the scene takes practice. Even when not speaking, it was important to focus on the speaker because the audience whose eyes would often wander would be drawn back to the main actor by other non-speaking actors. Without knowing any data, I would hazard a guess that "Help" is the most often uttered word in a prayer. When we are lost, trying to remember our purpose on this stage of life, we tend to look away for help. The help we long for is not out in the darkness, but in the main actor on the stage. Jesus is front and center. To look to him and order our days and our deeds around him is to re-discover our important role as disciple.

❖ ❖ ❖

Holy God, direct us and guide us as we follow you. Amen.

OCTOBER ◆ 20

2 Timothy 4:1-2
In the presence of God and of Christ Jesus, who is to judge the living and the dead, and in view of his appearing and his kingdom, I solemnly urge you: proclaim the message; be persistent whether the time is favorable or unfavorable; convince, rebuke, and encourage, with the utmost patience in teaching.

❖ ❖ ❖

Our lives are all about timing. It is never a good time for a flat tire or a head cold or a death in the family. We hope that time will bring answers, relief, hope, a different attitude, a better marriage, happier kids. Someday soon we will read that book we've wanted to read, take that trip, have that cup of coffee with a friend, fix that broken chair. The truth of who Christ is and longs to be for us is not a matter to be thrown into the winds of time. The only way to become a follower of Jesus Christ is to be a follower of Jesus Christ. Every day. All the time.

❖ ❖ ❖

Holy God, help us to seize this day which you have given us to proclaim your rule of justice and love. Amen.

OCTOBER ◆ 21

Luke 18:1
Then Jesus told them a parable about their need to pray always and not to lose heart.

❖ ❖ ❖

It reels the imagination that disciples who experienced Jesus up close and personal for about 4 years would ever have a problem remembering to pray or not losing heart. Perhaps Jesus was anticipating the time in the near future when the disciples would, in fact, lose heart. If the disciples can forget to pray and lose heart, then it shouldn't surprise us either. Our regional bishop often reminds congregations to pray for their pastors and remind their pastors to time the time for themselves to pray. Pastors are supposed to be purveyors of perpetual prayer, and yet we plow into the details of our day, get discouraged and have the audacity to wonder about God's whereabouts. Jesus told a parable about persistence in prayer so that we would not ever slip into thinking that God is not listening or that God doesn't care.

❖ ❖ ❖

Holy God, hear our prayer and hold our hearts so that this day we may live and hope in you. Amen.

OCTOBER ◆ 22

Luke 4:42
And when they reached him, they wanted to prevent him from leaving them.

❖   ❖   ❖

I have medicines in my cabinet for a runny nose, itchy eyes, and a nagging cough. They won't cure a cold but they will treat the symptoms. Keeping those medicines handy is a good idea. Treating the symptoms and not the disease is often our only course of action. We take medications to ease the symptoms while we wait for the cold to run its course. The people of God saw Jesus batting away demons and healing diseases. They wanted to keep him around to treat their symptoms from day to day. When we get into a mindset that treating the symptoms is the only thing to do, we lose sight of how big God is. Jesus had places to go, people to heal and God's word to proclaim, but it was all on the way to the cross. On the cross, Jesus cured the disease that condemned us to death. The symptoms of sin still linger but Jesus is more than a soothing cough medicine. Jesus is the Savior of our lives.

❖   ❖   ❖

Holy God, forgive us when we try to contain you and heal us that we might be free to serve. Amen.

OCTOBER ◆ 23

Jeremiah 31:33
But this is the covenant that I will make with the house of Israel after those days, says the Lord: I will put my law within them, and I will write it on their hearts; and I will be their God, and they shall be my people.

❖ ❖ ❖

We cannot function without some level of trust. We have to trust that people will do their jobs, keep their promises, follow through on their commitments. When such trust is eroded, then we have to build networks of accountability and those networks require attention and more levels of trust. The relationship which God established with his people required trust. Our part in that relationship broke down quickly, and yet God renewed it time after time. Even when we could not honor the promises, God honored the promised he made with us. God was not going to be denied a relationship with his people even when we prove ourselves to be untrustworthy. There will be a day when this relationship between God and his people is not so much work, especially for God.

❖ ❖ ❖

Bring it on, Lord, bring on the day when we can found trustworthy in your presence. Amen.

OCTOBER ◆ 24

Romans 1:28-32
And since they did not see fit to acknowledge God, God gave them up to a debased mind and to things that should not be done. They were filled with every kind of wickedness, evil, covetousness, malice. Full of envy, murder, strife, deceit, craftiness, they are gossips, slanderers, God-haters, insolent, haughty, boastful, inventors of evil, rebellious toward parents, foolish, faithless, heartless, ruthless. They know God's decree, that those who practice such things deserve to die-yet they not only do them but even applaud others who practice them.

❖   ❖   ❖

I was channel surfing last night through television programs that make me cringe. Shopping channels try to dazzle our money away from us for things we don't need. Infomercials hawk items that don't work. News channels are so hungry for news they create it out of thin air or chew on stories like an salivating dog. Evangelists make a handsome living off the income of those isolated from family and local communities. Comedies and dramas send our ability to laugh or be shocked into the depths of our own depravity. The state of the culture in the first century when this letter to the Roman Christians were written was not that much better than our own. Our best hope is not in changing the rules or even in obeying the letter of the law. It is in acknowledging God and our need for salvation. It is as simple and as difficult as that.

❖   ❖   ❖

Precious Lord, fill us with your Spirit that drives us ever closer to you. Amen.

OCTOBER ◆ 25

John 8:34
Jesus answered them, "Very truly, I tell you, everyone who commits sin is a slave to sin. The slave does not have a permanent place in the household; the son has a place there forever. So if the Son makes you free, you will be free indeed.

❖ ❖ ❖

Robert Frost once said that "Home is the place where, when you have to go there, they have to take you in." We all know that employers have their limits when it comes to our bad behavior. Families are the last resort for an open door and a bit of grace when we desperately need it. We also know that even families have their limits and certain levels of behavior cannot be tolerated without threatening the whole household. The miracle of God's house is that the door is always open, that there is always a space for grace and that the cross of Christ is strong enough to take on the worst we can throw at it. We are the fools for thinking that freedom lies outside the door instead of inside it.

❖ ❖ ❖

God of the open door, embrace us in all our foolishness and teach us your gracious ways. Amen.

OCTOBER ◆ 26

Mark 10:21
Jesus, looking at him, loved him and said, "You lack one thing..."

❖ ❖ ❖

In a discussion about the possibility that Jesus might be returning soon, one college student said "I don't want him to come too soon...I've got plans!" We all have something that would stand in the way of following Jesus with our whole lives. In Mark's story, the man was willing to serve but clinging too closely to his wealth for security. For the college student, his own future plans were more important than the future God had in store for him. The way of the cross requires us to reconsider that to which we cling so closely. Our hope for the future is at stake. No one else but Jesus can ask us to give up everything and follow him. One would hope that with someone as powerful as Jesus doing the asking, we would respond in a heartbeat. But the wealthy man showed us how difficult it is to let go even if the Savior of the world is asking. The impossibility of anyone being able to serve God completely looms. Jesus looked at the wealthy man and loved him and so he does us as well. There, in the love of Jesus, lies our best future.

❖ ❖ ❖

Holy God, thank you for your love. Help us to let go of that to which we cling too tightly. Amen.

OCTOBER ◆ 27

Daniel 7:13-14
As I watched in the night visions, I saw one like a human being coming with the clouds of heaven. And he came to the Ancient One and was presented before him. To him was given dominion and glory and kingship, that all peoples, nations, and languages should serve him. His dominion is an everlasting dominion that shall not pass away, and his kingship is one that shall never be destroyed.

❖ ❖ ❖

"Biblical proportions." That phrase has entered our vocabulary because so many of the stories and pictures of the scriptures are huge, grand, and majestic. Biblical images are filled with measurements from earth to heaven, from land to seas, all kingdoms and nations. All of it is to show the nature of God - that God is big...bigger than we can even imagine. But there are days when I am awash not with the grandeur of the world but in the details of daily life. I have great confidence in God's mastery of the universe, but I need to know where he is in the details when the details cannot be ignored or neatly prioritized. Too much attention to details can entrap us in a tyranny of urgency. In that tyranny, there might not be many good choices. So we dive into a vat of details in biblical proportions and trust that God will attend to the detail of each one of us.

❖ ❖ ❖

Lord God, hang on. Amen.

OCTOBER ◆ 28

Psalm 14:2
The Lord looks down from heaven on humankind to see if there are any who are wise, who seek after God.

❖   ❖   ❖

I truly appreciate the work of Stephen Hawking, the renowned theoretical physicist, whose keen and brilliant mind has opened so many doors of possibility regarding the nature of the universe. He has helped us to see stars and galaxies and everything in between in bold, new ways. He is using every gift to share his knowledge with the world. He takes offense to those who interrupt the scientific process by attempting to factor God into the equation regarding the origins of the universe. He takes flak for appearing to be anti-God. I do not see him so much as against God. Hawking is FOR science. The universe is a huge and mysterious place that scientists like Hawking are helping us to know. Those who seek after God will find him more accessible than even the incredible mysteries of science. Those who are wise will discover the depth and breadth of God's character in the passion of person for science.

❖   ❖   ❖

Holy God, reveal the wonders of the universe to us through the mind of your creations and the mystery of your heart. Amen.

OCTOBER ◆ 29

Ephesians 1:17-19
I pray that the God of our Lord Jesus Christ, the Father of glory, may give you a spirit of wisdom and revelation as you come to know him, so that, with the eyes of your heart enlightened, you may know what is the hope to which he has called you, what are the riches of his glorious inheritance among the saints, and what is the immeasurable greatness of his power for us who believe, according to the working of his great power.

❖   ❖   ❖

I have met people who are very smart. I have met people who have huge hearts. But the people that I admire greatly are those with smart hearts. The smart-hearted are those who walk through their lives with a willing balance between their heart and their head. Wisdom is uninformed without an understanding of the facts of our emotions. And to allow our emotions to run amok without sound thinking does little service to those around us. A smart heart knows the ways of the world and the power of love. It knows the magnitude of the grace of God.

❖   ❖   ❖

Holy God, enlighten our hearts with your wisdom and infect our minds with your compassion. Amen.

OCTOBER ◆ 30

Isaiah 53:5-6
But he was wounded for our transgressions, crushed for our iniquities; upon him was the punishment that made us whole, and by his bruises we are healed. All we like sheep have gone astray; we have all turned to our own way, and the Lord has laid on him the iniquity of us all.

❖ ❖ ❖

It is morning. I am staring at this Isaiah passage which graphically and profoundly speaks of the sacrifice that the Savior of the world will make and did make. It speaks of those whose sins have driven the necessity of such a savior. But it is morning and my mind, though compelled to linger inside the power of the prophet's words, drifts quickly to the pressing questions of the day...most of the questions start with, "What must I do about......" Jesus is forgotten in the blur of the urgent. The passage promises wholeness, but I focus on broken pieces. The passage promises healing, but I continue to deny the disease of my own self-centeredness that strangles me. We have all known a lifetime of mornings and even still, Jesus meets us where we are and bids us let his cross consume our anxiety, fear and restlessness so that we can be free again. The grace proclaimed in the darkness of the cross is food for the hungriest soul in the light of each new day.

❖ ❖ ❖

Precious Lord, we follow you into this week with gratitude and hope. Amen.

OCTOBER ◆ 31

I John 3:7
Little children, let no one deceive you. Everyone who does what is right is righteous, just as he is righteous.

❖   ❖   ❖

One Halloween I saw several dozen kids decked out in their costumes. Among the crowd there was Batman, Batwoman, SpongeBob, a mermaid, a ghost or two, a football player, one of Sherwood Forest's merry men and several princesses. The world can be a scary and deceptive place. Halloween is our tongue-in-cheek effort to laugh at what scares us and to wear masks rather than be frightened by them. We take steps in our growth not to be so afraid of the dark that we are paralyzed. We fight our fear best by knowing and doing what is right and trusting God through the day and the night.

❖   ❖   ❖

Holy God, guide us in the way of light and truth. Amen.

NOVEMBER ◆ 1

John 6:67-69
So Jesus asked the Twelve, "Do you also wish to go away?" Simon Peter answered him, "Lord, to whom can we go?" You have the words of eternal life. We have come to believe and know that you are the Holy One of God.

❖ ❖ ❖

There is a scene in the movie "An Officer and a Gentleman" where the drill instructor is working feverishly to break an officer candidate of his self-serving behaviors or quit the program. When the instructor screams in the candidate's face to get him to quit, the candidate finally drops his emotional wall and says, "No...No....I have nowhere else to go." It may not be the most rousing statement of commitment, but it is a keen awareness of one's condition. Even in those moments of deepest doubt, angst and frustration in our relationship with God...the alternatives are lifeless compared to the powerful promise of a loving God.

❖ ❖ ❖

Precious Lord, we are fickled children who easily run away from you. Help us always to know the way home. Amen.

NOVEMBER ◆ 2

Deuteronomy 4:9
But take care and watch yourselves closely, so as neither to forget the things that your eyes have seen nor to let them slip from your mind all the days of your life; make them known

❖ ❖ ❖

We forget a lot. We forget names and faces and numbers and appointments and why we went to the store. A good part of the problem of our relationship with God is that we forget. We fill our heads with other clutter and important stuff. God's presence and purpose becomes lost in the blizzard of post-a-notes. We can forget ourselves too. Either way, we are truly lost. God remembers us by name and in moments of clarity and peace we may hear it. God continues to remind us of his love and grace even in the midst of the din of our days.

❖ ❖ ❖

Stir our memories, Lord, with the thousands of times you have nudged us back to life. Amen.

NOVEMBER ◆ 3

Daniel 12:3
Those who are wise shall shine like the brightness of the sky, and those who lead many to righteousness, like the stars forever and ever.

❖   ❖   ❖

Often I ask people how or when did their faith life have a noticeable growth spurt? The stories that follow are almost always about a person who made Christ real for them through an act of kindness, an inspiring word, a gentle spirit, or a selfless act. We have the power to influence one another so that our lives become more a testimony to the light than a canvas for the darkness. Incarnate means to embody in the flesh - to take an idea or dream and make it real - tangible - touchable. Those who help others touch and see love are blessed indeed.

❖   ❖   ❖

Holy God, take my life and let it be always, only, all for thee. Amen.

NOVEMBER ◆ 4

Psalm 96:1-3
O sing to the Lord a new song; sing to the Lord, all the earth. Sing to the Lord, bless his name; tell of his salvation from day to day. Declare his glory among the nations, his marvelous works among all the peoples.

❖   ❖   ❖

After the terrorist attacks on 9/11, I preached about the dangers of worshipping the "god of normal." We all desperately wanted life to be normal again. After any long, often painful process, we want normal days again. We want normal more than anything. After a hurricane struck our area, we longed for normal. We all want a normal stock market. Nothing can completely return to where it was before the disaster struck. There is a normal, but it is a new normal. It takes shape whether we like it or not and it will be in place until something else comes along to knock that god of normal off the mountain. The Lord of our lives is the one constant and his purposes are being revealed every day. Rather than longing for normal, the energy of longing better spent on a new song for the "God who is our help in ages past and our hope for years to come."

❖   ❖   ❖

Almighty God, you are shaping a new world. Help us to see it and trust in your unfailing love. Amen.

NOVEMBER ◆ 5

I Thessalonians 1:2-5
We always give thanks to God for all of you and mention you in our prayers, constantly remembering before our God and Father your work of faith and labor of love and steadfastness of hope in our Lord Jesus Christ. For we know, brothers and sisters beloved by God, that he has chosen you, because our message of the gospel came to you not in word only, but also in power and in the Holy Spirit and with full conviction; just as you know what kind of persons we proved to be among you for your sake.

❖ ❖ ❖

Early in my career, I had a conversation with a colleague who had a child with severe, life-long disabilities. In an effort to say something encouraging and supportive, I said that he and his wife must be remarkable people for God to have chosen them for this little one. His response was curt and angry. The notion of being chosen by God was no comfort or help to him. I quickly apologized for making assumptions about his feelings. I learned that the art of encouragement is more complicated. Saying words just for the sake of saying something or making a good "cookie cutter" comment rarely ever helps and can do more damage. Some are encouraged by knowing they are not alone. Others are encouraged by clarity of vision. Still others are helped by knowing that they are playing a crucial role in a larger purpose for the greater good. Sometimes just thanking God for one another and praying for one another is good.

❖ ❖ ❖

Give us the grace and wisdom to know how to lift one another up and share one another's burdens. Amen.

NOVEMBER ◆ 6

Matthew 22:15-17
Then the Pharisees went and plotted to entrap him in what he said. So they sent their disciples to him, along with the Herodians, saying, "Teacher, we know that you are sincere, and teach the way of God in accordance with truth, and show deference to no one; for you do not regard people with partiality. Tell us, then, what you think. Is it lawful to pay taxes to the emperor, or not?"

❖   ❖   ❖

Political candidates complain about the media's "Gotcha" questions which are posed to intentionally expose a candidate's lack of knowledge or area of weakness as if this is anything new. "Gotcha" questions have been around since the creation of human beings and God really invented them, "So Adam & Eve.....who told you that you were naked?" The Pharisees came armed with "gotcha" questions for the purpose of exposing Jesus and bringing him down. God comes armed with "Gotcha" questions for the purpose of restoring our relationship. Therein lies the difference.

❖   ❖   ❖

Holy God, we confess to you our weakness and sin and trust in the power of your restoring grace. Amen.

NOVEMBER ◆ 7

Isaiah 35:6-7
Then the lame shall leap like a deer, and the tongue of the speechless sing for joy. For the waters shall break forth in the wilderness, and streams in the desert; the burning sand shall become a pool, and the thirsty ground springs of water.

❖   ❖   ❖

To the people of God who were weak in the face of strong oppression, the prophet's words of hope were like a drink of cool water on a hot day. The vision of people made whole and thirst quenched is a tangible image of a God who cares intimately for the us. Sometimes even in the midst of dry times, we can drink the words of promise and find satisfaction in the taste of hope.

❖   ❖   ❖

God of hope, may we be the vessel for your refreshing spirit. Amen.

NOVEMBER ◆ 8

Jeremiah 31:34
No longer shall they teach one another, or say to each other, "Know the Lord," for they shall all know me, from the least of them to the greatest, says the Lord; for I will forgive their iniquity, and remember their sin no more.

❖ ❖ ❖

The moments of forgiveness are the defining moments of relationships. Our memories are vulnerable to lack of nurture or aging tissues. What lingers, however, is the knowledge of unconditional love. Love is a muscle that atrophies when taken for granted. It flexes with suffering and hurt and prevails in the struggle when forgiving. Such is the nature of our God. If we know nothing else about this God than this is the One who forgives, we have the memory we most need.

❖ ❖ ❖

Holy God, the best of who you are can be seen when you forgive us at our worst. Amen.

NOVEMBER ◆ 9

Luke 6:27-29
But I say to you that listen, Love your enemies, do good to those who hate you, bless those who curse you, pray for those who abuse you. If anyone strikes you on the cheek, offer the other also; and from anyone who takes away your coat do not withhold even your shirt.

❖ ❖ ❖

The woman came sheepishly into my office. She fiddled with her hands. She rarely looked up at me. Her presenting issue was that she was trying to understand this Bible verse about loving your enemy and turning the other cheek. She wanted to know if it meant that Christians should be doormats. The word "doormat" set lights flashing in my head that there was more going on here than a quibble with scripture. As it turned out, she was being beaten by her husband. The hard reality of this verse is that the enemy rarely means an opponent in a far off country. It means the people with whom we live. No, it does not reduce us to doormats on which others may cruelly wipe their shoes. No, it doesn't say that hitting back is the best response either. It does say that we must meet acts of hate with acts of love. In abusive relationships, the most loving act is to leave, to walk away, and yes, sometimes the most loving thing to do is to end a relationship. For those of us who endure the slings and arrows of lesser battles, we can turn the other cheek and still be alive to live and love another day.

❖ ❖ ❖

Lord God, help us not to be the enemy that someone is having to work so hard to love. Amen.

NOVEMBER ◆ 10

Romans 1:16-17
For I am not ashamed of the gospel; it is the power of God for salvation to everyone who has faith, to the Jew first and also to the Greek. For in it the righteousness of God is revealed through faith for faith; as it is written, "The one who is righteous will live by faith."

❖ ❖ ❖

I saw a documentary that was presented in a humorous manner to mock all people who have any religious belief. It was easy for the film makers to identify religious people who look outrageously silly. People of faith are not without those who tend to latch on to one peculiar aspect and who look like buffoons in public. It also begs the question of whether they are prompting faith or hungering for attention. The Gospel itself contains the foolishness of unconditional love. Grace does not follow any rules of fairness or logic, and yet, for those who believe it is freedom and life. To live as Christians we must choose to put aside the ridicule as graciously as we have been forgiven when we have criticized others. We as humans are quite adept at criticizing one another to bits, but God still offers a way of salvation that withstands our slings and arrows.

❖ ❖ ❖

Holy God, we boldly claim that you are Lord and thank you for the faith that you have stirred up in us. Amen.

NOVEMBER ◆ 11

John 8:34-36
Jesus answered them, "Very truly, I tell you, everyone who commits sin is a slave to sin. The slave does not have a permanent place in the household; the son has a place there forever. So if the Son makes you free, you will be free indeed.

❖   ❖   ❖

I have to remind myself regularly that I am free not to be messy. Without thinking about it too much, I can be a slave to some sloppy habits. I have the will and the way to attend to my chores so that my world - at least the part of it over which I have any real control - is ordered and neat. From day to day, we need to be reminded to be free children of the living God rather than slaves to the sin that seduces us into believing that we are only human. We evoke that designation of "only human" as an excuse for being wrong. God meant it to be something a bit more wonderful.

❖   ❖   ❖

Holy God, remind us today who we are because of you. Amen.

NOVEMBER ◆ 12

Daniel 7:14
To him was given dominion and glory and kingship, that all peoples, nations, and languages should serve him. His dominion is an everlasting dominion that shall not pass away, and his kingship is one that shall never be destroyed.

❖ ❖ ❖

When Daniel was having visions, it came at a time after rabbis and priests had been driven from the temple in Jerusalem. The temple space was then used for sacrifices to Greek gods. The morale of God's people was crushed. They needed a new mental image to keep them from the pits of despair. Daniel's prophetic dreams gave them hope. These days, prophetic images - even if they do come from Hollywood - paint bleak pictures of the future and the only hope rests on the human spirit to endure and prevail. Martin Luther said that if he knew that the world would end tomorrow, he would plant a tree. So powerful is hope when it is born even from dreams and visions, it lives on what is true about the faithfulness of God.

❖ ❖ ❖

Almighty and ever-living God, we move hopefully through each day because of you. Amen.

NOVEMBER ◆ 13

Revelation 7:15-17
For this reason they are before the throne of God, and worship him day and night within his temple, and the one who is seated on the throne will shelter them. They will hunger no more, and thirst no more; the sun will not strike them, nor any scorching heat; for the Lamb at the center of the throne will be their shepherd, and he will guide them to springs of the water of life, and God will wipe away every tear from their eyes."

❖ ❖ ❖

There is much in the book of Revelation that makes for a feast of speculation about the future. Those who like to dissect minute details in symbols and images have much to work with and can confuse as much as they try to clarify. Revelation was written at a time of great suffering and persecution. The images of a God who triumphs like a giant warrior and who wipes tears away as a tender shepherd were gifts to a hurting people so that they would persevere in their faith. It must have worked. Hundreds of years since the time of their suffering, we are a people who have heard the word of life in Jesus Christ because of their faithfulness in witness. May we be less caught up with fear and speculation and more courageous for the sake of all who will come after us.

❖ ❖ ❖

Holy God, for all the saints who have suffered and died keeping the faith, we thank you for their enduring discipleship. Amen.

NOVEMBER ◆ 14

Psalm 34:8-10
O taste and see that the Lord is good; happy are those who take refuge in him. O fear the Lord, you his holy ones, for those who fear him have no want. The young lions suffer want and hunger, but those who seek the Lord lack no good thing.

❖   ❖   ❖

When I asked a person to bring snacks for an upcoming meeting, she asked "Sweet or salty?" I had to stop and think about what time of the day the meeting was going to be, if it was close to a meal or after. Our taste buds seem to have minds of their own. I stand in front of my refrigerator or pantry and ask the question, "What am I hungry for?" Of course, I am rarely hungry for something GOOD for me! It takes some thinking beyond my fickled taste buds to eat what is actually good for the whole body. A life of faith begins by having faith. A relationship with Jesus Christ is always a good thing. Taste and see.

❖   ❖   ❖

Precious Lord, for your nurturing care we give you thanks. Amen.

NOVEMBER ◆ 15

Psalm 121:8
The Lord will keep your going out and your coming in from this time on and forevermore.

❖   ❖   ❖

I don't remember much of the Greek I studied in seminary anymore. I have to look up and re-learn to teach it and preach it. Truth be told, I didn't remember much during my Greek exams either! I do, however, remember the verb - ἔρχομαι - which means both coming and going. I think it stood out for me because it sounded like a great truth beyond just a simple word. We are a people who are coming and going. Parents have their most significant conversations with their children in the car on the way to or from some activity. We have to leave one meeting early to arrive late for another meeting. We graze through our meals more than sit down to dinner. The idea that we could possibly be kept, protected and served in the midst of all that - ἔρχομαι - boggles the mind. But God is the God of our coming and going.

❖   ❖   ❖

Help us to remember, Lord, that even as you are chasing us, you are never out of breath. Amen.

NOVEMBER ◆ 16

Numbers 11: 27-29
And a young man ran and told Moses, "Eldad and Medad are prophesying in the camp." And Joshua son of Nun, the assistant of Moses, one of his chosen men, said, "My lord, Moses, stop them!" But Moses said to him, "Are you jealous for my sake? Would that all the Lord's people were prophets, and that the Lord would put his spirit on them!"

❖ ❖ ❖

There is a part of us which would love to be on the inside track, be "in-the-know," have a corner on the truth. God makes his spirit and his truth readily available to all and also gives us the ability to discern the truth in matters vital to our faith. We, however, might try to silence the speakers of God's truth out of our misguided notion that only we can protect the integrity of God's word. We are called to recognize the truth when we hear it, rejoice in it and speak it ourselves as the spirit gives us guidance. In the business of making Christ known, the more the merrier.

❖ ❖ ❖

Holy God, forgive us when try to contain your spirit and help us find the grace to work for your kingdom together. Amen.

NOVEMBER ◆ 17

Luke 6:27-31
"But I say to you that listen, Love your enemies, do good to those who hate you, bless those who curse you, pray for those who abuse you. If anyone strikes you on the cheek, offer the other also; and from anyone who takes away your coat do not withhold even your shirt. Give to everyone who begs from you; and if anyone takes away your goods, do not ask for them again. Do to others as you would have them do to you.

❖   ❖   ❖

We do and say things that annoy, hurt, anger and ruffle other people. It happens all the time. We need to ask for forgiveness, confess our sins and heal the breach those words and actions have created. That takes work. That takes wanting to have a decent relationship with the one we have offended. We decide that it would be easier to maintain them as an enemy than forgive what they do or say. That makes sense to us. Jesus says, love them anyway. We are called to forgive one another and to love our enemies. Either way, it is work. We get to choose the work of healing a friendship or caring for an enemy. It is the only way to live in peace inside our own skin.

❖   ❖   ❖

Holy God, soften our hearts and turn us toward one another and away from our own self-interest. Amen.

NOVEMBER ◆ 18

Joel 2:26
You shall eat in plenty and be satisfied, and praise the name of the Lord your God, who dealt wondrously with you. And my people shall never again be put to shame.

❖ ❖ ❖

I have a dog and a parrot. The dog does not like it when I raise my voice. She has flash-backs of her puppy days of chewing everything in sight. When she hears my loud voice, she tuck her tail and cowers even when she isn't doing anything wrong. She has only two states of mind - joy and shame. My bird, however, knows no shame. Even when I try to shame him, he mocks me with my own words, "Bad Bird, Bad Bird." Too much shame is paralyzing and too little is naive and aggravating because we would all love to live without shame. The day will come, says the Lord, when we will be wondrously treated and never be shamed. In God's heart, that day is today. We can live inside that day by offering that joy and freedom to one another.

❖ ❖ ❖

Holy God, free us from the shame of our sinfulness and help us rest alive and free in your presence. Amen.

NOVEMBER ◆ 19

Jeremiah 31:13
Then shall the young women rejoice in the dance, and the young men and the old shall be merry. I will turn their mourning into joy, I will comfort them, and give them gladness for sorrow.

❖ ❖ ❖

The words of the prophet are ancient. We have the words on pieces of dried parchment. Copies made on pages that are brittle to the point of dust. And yet, these words of promise spring up and quench dead roots, shriveled branches, wilted flowers, and give the earth a pulse again so vibrant that it makes a sound. We have all known moments of overflowing joy. We will even laugh by ourselves or smile alone in a room to make sure our faces remember what to do. We can't avoid or ignore the circumstances that cause the sorrows, but we can keeping taking the dancing lessons and trust that the music that we sometimes hear only timidly in the farthest reaches of our hearts will be loud enough for everyone to hear. God is singing to us.

❖ ❖ ❖

Holy God, teach us how to dance to prepare for your kingdom. Amen.

NOVEMBER ◆ 20

Psalm 17:13,15
Rise up, O Lord, confront them, overthrow them! By your sword deliver my life from the wicked.....As for me, I shall behold your face in righteousness; when I awake I shall be satisfied, beholding your likeness.

❖ ❖ ❖

The psalms are filled with the emotional struggles of those in a position of leadership. Sleep is lost. Anxiety is high. Prayers are rants of frustration that the evil consistently have their way while the righteous are punished. Almost always there are threads of faith and trust and hope that are woven throughout and whose pattern prevails. The final picture to be reveals in the tangle mass is one of a face. Something there is about finding home in the eyes of the one who loves us.

❖ ❖ ❖

Holy God, we trust in your presence and long for your face. Amen.

NOVEMBER ◆ 21

2 Thessalonians:16-17
Now may our Lord Jesus Christ himself and God our Father, who loved us and through grace gave us eternal comfort and good hope, comfort your hearts and strengthen them in every good work and word.

❖   ❖   ❖

No matter our age, we never outgrow our need for comfort. As a child, it is as simple as a familiar blanket, a warm embrace, a soothing voice. As adults, we deny our need and often mindlessly adopt unhealthy habits to fill a void. It takes great faith maturity to admit our need for love. We make our lives more complicated than they need to be. It is through a loving act or a kind word that we are blanketed with the undeserved love of God. Good works and good words strengthen weary hearts and the grace of God in Christ is eternally familiar.

❖   ❖   ❖

Holy God, surround us with your comfort and hope and use us to comfort others. Amen.

NOVEMBER ◆ 22

Luke 20:38
Now he is God not of the dead, but of the living; for to him all of them are alive.

❖ ❖ ❖

We spend probably too much time thinking about "the other side." Heaven or hell. Life after death. Who is going to get in? What will it look like? All we know for certain is that Jesus will be there and through the grace of God, we will be there and we will be very much alive. I suspect the greatest moment of discomfort will be realizing how much time we wasted in this life fretting about something so eternal and so wonderful.

❖ ❖ ❖

Holy God, we fling ourselves into this day and trust you with eternity. Amen.

NOVEMBER ◆ 23

Luke 10:38-40a
Now as they went on their way, he entered a certain village, where a woman named Martha welcomed him into her home. She had a sister named Mary, who sat at the Lord's feet and listened to what he was saying. But Martha was distracted by her many tasks

❖ ❖ ❖

One of my favorite t-shirt slogans says, "Jesus is coming! Look busy." I had a conversation recently that involved defining American culture and a key component of the definition was "working." Employment is crucial for the health of our families and communities. Losing a job is like being kicked in the gut and shoved to the side of a road on which the traffic is moving uncomfortably fast. Parents have time to read a book or listen to music or have friends, but they have to steal the time from work, or household responsibilities or sleep to make it happen, if at all. One wonders when we will all reach our tipping points and say, "Enough!" The writer Frederick Buechner said that it is often in those moments when we get away, drive to the beach, listen to a symphony in which we find our salvation again. Mary had reached her tipping point, perhaps, and decided to sit and listen to Jesus. We can either call her to get back to work, envy her or take her lead.

❖ ❖ ❖

Hi, Lord, have a seat. Talk to me. Amen.

NOVEMBER ◆ 24

Luke 1:39-40
In those days Mary set out and went with haste to a Judean town in the hill country, where she entered the house of Zechariah and greeted Elizabeth.

❖ ❖ ❖

It is the time of year when people are making plans to travel to spend time with family. Relationships need face time even if it only happens sporadically during the week or the years. Time spent with one another won't magically make problems disappear, but the face time does give relationship what they need to grow. I have a Christmas cactus that I regularly ignore. It decorates my house - it does everything I want and expect it to do and it only needs a little water once in a while. Certainly relationships need more, but to ignore the most basic needs - face time - is to strain it beyond recovery. Mary and Elizabeth prepared for the Kingdom of God simply by spending time with each other. To grow in our relationship with God may be just that simple.

❖ ❖ ❖

Holy God, may we see your face today in one another. Amen.

November ◆ 25

Psalm 98:4-5
Make a joyful noise to the Lord, all the earth; break forth into joyous song and sing praises.
Sing praises to the Lord with the lyre, with the lyre and the sound of melody.

❖   ❖   ❖

Children make noise. They run through the halls of our church. They bang on the walls. Some cry when their parents leave them and some squeal in the playground. They make noise. They just like being alive and aren't yet equipped with all the vocabulary to express themselves in more sedate ways and so they make noise. We are wise to remember that we are just children in the Kingdom of God and we have permission to sing and make music and even some noise to give praise to God just for the joy of being alive.

❖   ❖   ❖

Lord God, let all the noises we make today be joyfully expressed in your direction. Amen.

NOVEMBER ◆ 26

2 Thessalonians 3:11-13
For we hear that some of you are living in idleness, mere busybodies, not doing any work. Now such persons we command and exhort in the Lord Jesus Christ to do their work quietly and to earn their own living. Brothers and sisters, do not be weary in doing what is right.

❖   ❖   ❖

I can imagine the Apostle Paul getting the news via messenger from the church at Thessalonica. There was internal strife. Members speaking ill of other members. There were jealous rants and nitpicking over who was or wasn't doing whatever. It is the stuff that probably made Paul want to run screaming from the room. Given the larger issues he was facing and death itself, the news of the people of God being painfully human was no doubt discouraging. Paul knew that despite the setbacks and people who insisted on living small lives that he still believed in Jesus and in us enough to call us back to the right stuff.

❖   ❖   ❖

Lord God, may we be bearers not of criticism but of the Good News. Amen.

NOVEMBER ◆ 27

Luke 21:14-15
So make up your minds not to prepare your defense in advance; for I will give you words and a wisdom that none of your opponents will be able to withstand or contradict.

❖ ❖ ❖

There are days I envy those of a theological mindset who believe their faith is best lived out by rigidly adhering to rules of behavior and telling other people to follow those rules. It is the neatness and simplicity that I envy. When a person is sitting in front of me for guidance after making a complete mess of their lives, it would be so easy to point out their sin and write a nice ,neat, prescriptive solution of "get your life right with God." When I open my mouth though, I am reminded of the God who didn't wait for me to get things right to die for me and love me back to life. I hear words of forgiveness and grace. I am grateful for the God who puts the right words in my mouth instead of letting my own fly out.

❖ ❖ ❖

Holy God, may the words of my mouth bring messages of grace. Amen.

NOVEMBER ◆ 28

Mark 11:25
Whenever you stand praying, forgive, if you have anything against anyone.

❖   ❖   ❖

An old rock song included the question "How can love survive in such a graceless age?" We all have built within us a dream of what love can be. It is wired into our synapses of our brains and woven into our genetic code. But buried beneath our selfish nature, it remains a dream to many or appears only fleetingly to others. We love in flashes and moments, but have difficulty sustaining it. Jesus knew that love cannot survive in a graceless age. Love needs forgiveness to survive. We need forgiveness to be at one with ourselves, our God and God's people. We cannot even pretend to hold the dream of love without the capacity to restore the love when it is broken. Christ's mission on the cross was so that love could be more than a dream. He bids his disciples to forgive one another and pray. By doing so we cannot bring on the Kingdom any sooner than God is ready to do so, but in forgiving we lean in each other direction and get a glimpse of God's dream for us all.

❖   ❖   ❖

Holy God, forgive us as we forgive. Grant us a glimpse of your Kingdom come. Amen.

November ◆ 29

Jeremiah 23:3-4
Then I myself will gather the remnant of my flock out of all the lands where I have driven them, and I will bring them back to their fold, and they shall be fruitful and multiply. I will raise up shepherds over them who will shepherd them, and they shall not fear any longer, or be dismayed, nor shall any be missing, says the Lord.

❖ ❖ ❖

One part of the job description of the Holy Spirit is to create and maintain the Church. When the human ego is let loose, we have a tendency to think that we are in the saving business, that we are the ones saving souls, that we are the ones keeping the Church alive. That is all fine and good until we are the ones who need the saving. Throughout the history of the people of Israel, God has gathered, maintained and nurtured his people. Time and time again God has stirred a faithful remnant that have been the active leaven for a new people. We are here this day because God does not give up.

❖ ❖ ❖

Lord, we gather together to ask for your blessing and to stir us to faithfulness. Amen.

NOVEMBER ◆ 30

Philippians 1:3-6
I thank my God every time I remember you, constantly praying with joy in every one of my prayers for all of you, because of your sharing in the gospel from the first day until now. I am confident of this, that the one who began a good work among you will bring it to completion by the day of Jesus Christ.

❖   ❖   ❖

I have unfinished chores and projects scattered throughout my house. Dishes in the sink. Bills to pay. Laundry to be done. Woodcarving projects in various stages of undoneness. Writing projects sitting in a computer hard drive ignored. At work, the list is longer - more urgent, more related to the needs of others, more overwhelming at times. Paul's gentle encouragement to the Philippians reminds me that it was God that sparked my life and invited me into these precious chores. It is God who is at work in me and who will be the one to put the finishing touches not only on my projects but on my life. Thanks be to God.

❖   ❖   ❖

I can do all things, Lord, with your precious company and by your strength. Amen.

DECEMBER ◆ 1

Isaiah 2:2-3
In days to come the mountain of the Lord's house shall be established as the highest of the mountains, and shall be raised above the hills; all the nations shall stream to it. Many peoples shall come and say, "Come, let us go up to the mountain of the Lord, to the house of the God of Jacob; that he may teach us his ways and that we may walk in his paths." For out of Zion shall go forth instruction, and the word of the Lord from Jerusalem.

❖ ❖ ❖

The debate among present day Christians continues to rumble about whether or not the mega-church is truly a good thing. Those outside of it are critical; those within it appreciate the program options and the power of multiple resources. Those in smaller, struggling churches look with a jealous eye toward the numbers of people, but often will sacrifice cherished traditions over the possibility of new members. There are a few communities that are able to do both, but deep resources of finances and personnel make it happen. As the Advent season begins, we are challenged to point ourselves toward the Good News of Jesus Christ and listen to his word. We will do this from gatherings big and small, in weak congregations and program-rich places. None of us is any closer to the kingdom of God than another. But all who bear the name of Christ lean in his direction and pray for the coming of the Lord who will eventually and forever bring us together.

❖ ❖ ❖

Come, Lord Jesus, come and hasten the day when we will worship you together in peace. Amen.

DECEMBER ◆ 2

Psalm 122:6-9
Pray for the peace of Jerusalem: "May they prosper who love you. Peace be within your walls, and security within your towers." or the sake of my relatives and friends I will say, "Peace be within you." For the sake of the house of the Lord our God, I will seek your good.

❖ ❖ ❖

Despite all the criticism that gets leveled at the Christmas season as being commercial or filled with hypocrisy, I think it is a wonderful opportunity to knock off some of the rough edges we have developed through the year. We enter into a time of awareness of our part in being peacemakers in a troubled world. We practice peace when we pray for one another especially for the one who is annoying us. We practice peace when we work at bringing out the best in one another instead of evoking the worst. We practice peace when we walk away from our anger and find ways to lift one another up. Christmas is work and prayer.

❖ ❖ ❖

Holy God, make us instruments of thy peace. Amen.

DECEMBER ◆ 3

Romans 13:11-12
Besides this, you know what time it is, how it is now the moment for you to wake from sleep. For salvation is nearer to us now than when we became believers; the night is far gone, the day is near. Let us then lay aside the works of darkness and put on the armor of light

❖ ❖ ❖

Bad, self-serving habits slink into our lives in the cover of darkness. If they arrived with noise at the front door, we would be smart enough to slam the door in their face. But the sloppy habits drift into our living spaces like cold air radiating through windows. As we prepare for the Christ Child, we need to take the famous hard looks at the way we move through the hours of our days. We have an opportunity to reflect the light of Christ's love and grace. Light on a dull surface goes nowhere. The time is now to wake from the sleep of our clutter and walk as children of light.

❖ ❖ ❖

Holy God, shine on us and help us to reflect your light to others. Amen.

DECEMBER ◆ 4

Matthew 24:42-44
Keep awake therefore, for you do not know on what day your Lord is coming. But understand this: if the owner of the house had known in what part of the night the thief was coming, he would have stayed awake and would not have let his house be broken into. Therefore you also must be ready, for the Son of Man is coming at an unexpected hour.

❖   ❖   ❖

Wouldn't that be somethin'? Imagine Jesus plopping himself down in whatever space you happen to be in right now. I wonder if he would fuss about the noise in the hallways or the temperature of the room? Would he drum his fingers with me because the computer seems slow in booting up this morning? Would he be fashioning a "to-do" list for the day? Have you ever had those moments of interruption when the world seemed to fall away and all that existed in that moment was the person in front of you and everything seemed to say, "it will all be all right." Though I admit I would probably be startled to have Jesus sitting in one of my office chairs right now, I would cherish the peace I would know in the "all-rightness" of that blessed company.

❖   ❖   ❖

Blessed Lord, enter into the din of our days with the peace that passes all understanding. Amen.

DECEMBER ♦ 5

Luke 4:28
When they heard this, all in the synagogue were filled with rage.

❖   ❖   ❖

When the people heard Jesus read the scriptures in the synagogue they probably smiled politely. When Jesus sat down and started to teach about the scriptures, the people heard hopeful news and started to get curious about this guy. But when Jesus said that the types of people they most despised understood God's will better than they did, they blew up. God's people were faithfully attending synagogue and hearing the scriptures and they got angry that Jesus would imply that someone less faithful could understand God's purposes better. The people listening in the synagogue had lost touch with their own deepest need for forgiveness and mercy. Jesus implied that sometimes those whom we would assume were the most clueless about God are closer to the truth than we are. It is not because they are smarter or that we are wrong. Understanding the scriptures requires not history of church attendance or theological mind, but simply the desire of a hungry heart.

❖   ❖   ❖

Lord, you satisfy the hungry heart with the food of your word made flesh. Amen.

DECEMBER ◆ 6

Genesis 2:7-8
Then the eyes of both were opened, and they knew that they were naked; and they sewed fig leaves together and made loincloths for themselves. They heard the sound of the Lord God walking in the garden at the time of the evening breeze, and the man and his wife hid themselves from the presence of the Lord God among the trees of the garden.

❖ ❖ ❖

    Comic ELOGOS response: Shopping is invented.

    Ironic ELOGOS response: Shoplifting is invented.

    Pessimistic ELOGOS response: ....and it all went downhill from there.

    Personal ELOGOS response: Difficult to imagine a time when nakedness ever looked good on anyone.

    Faithful ELOGOS response: God is looking for us.

❖ ❖ ❖

We are here, Lord, we are here. Amen.

DECEMBER ◆ 7

I Corinthians 1:30-31
He is the source of your life in Christ Jesus, who became for us wisdom from God, and righteousness and sanctification and redemption, in order that, as it is written, Let the one who boasts, boast in the Lord.

❖ ❖ ❖

God is "the source of your life." I think, "Well, that's a no-brainer....what else could be the source of one's life?" There are those who might say that their children are the source of their lives. Hard to argue with that. Not having any children, I try to lay low in those conversations lest I say something incredibly stupid. Children do give life meaning and purpose. They certainly demand a lot, too. We do like to boast about them whether it is how quickly they caught on to potty-training or what college they were accepted into. Rightly so. But I will tiptoe out into the waters of questioning our children as the source of life. The best parents I know are people who understand that their children do not ultimately exist to serve a purpose for them - their children exist as a gift, a blessing and a surprise with lots of strings of responsibility attached. The best thing we can do for our children and for ourselves is to understand that the source of life is not something we drain from one another, but we freely receive from God.

❖ ❖ ❖

Father, we adore you. Lay our lives before you. How we love you! Amen.

DECEMBER ◆ 8

Mark 10:20-21
He said to him, "Teacher, I have kept all these [commandments] since my youth." Jesus, looking at him, loved him and said, "You lack one thing; go, sell what you own, and give the money to the poor, then come, follow me."

❖ ❖ ❖

The radical nature of following Christ is certainly the key message of this text, but we miss something vital when we ignore "Jesus...loved him" Even though Jesus clearly understood the great obstacle of this man's attachment to his money and property, he did not let that be an obstacle for his love. Given the number of things I throw at God to make it more difficult to love me, it is good to know that God somehow finds a way to love me in spite of myself.

❖ ❖ ❖

Holy God, give us the courage to love beyond our comfort level. Amen.

DECEMBER ◆ 9

Mark 10:43
But it is not so among you; but whoever wishes to become great among you must be your servant, and whoever wishes to be first among you must be slave of all. For the Son of Man came not to be served but to serve, and to give his life a ransom for many.

❖   ❖   ❖

The little community of the disciples with Jesus fully and physically present was still vulnerable to the powers of dissention and discord in the ranks. People muscle for position to make themselves feel better. Over and over again they heard the message and we hear the message - "It is not about you." When we trust ourselves to the loving and merciful care of our Savior, we would be startled by how much time and energy we have available to us for others.

❖   ❖   ❖

Holy God, may our trust in you be so complete that we spend our days believing in your grace and working for justice. Amen.

DECEMBER ◆ 10

Zephaniah 1:7
Be silent before the Lord God! For the day of the Lord is at hand; the Lord has prepared a sacrifice, he has consecrated his guests.

❖   ❖   ❖

I was a guest speaker for a current class at the seminary I had attended years ago. I was anxious to dive into my talk and the discussion. The class, however, began with a time of silence. Given the frantic, exhausted manner in which students and teachers often enter classrooms, it was good to be provided a moment to re-center and focus on the task at hand. Into one moment we bring the baggage from the moments before and the moments to come. Silence for many is a luxury. To be silent before the Lord is more than a respectful gesture, it is a willful act of courage to trust God completely with that moment. It takes work to put aside all that which is pin-balling inside our heads and be completely present to the God who has been waiting an eternity for this moment with us.

❖   ❖   ❖

Holy God, quiet our minds and hearts so that we may feast in your presence. Amen.

December ◆ 11

Psalm 123:2-3
As the eyes of servants look to the hand of their master, as the eyes of a maid to the hand of her mistress, so our eyes look to the Lord our God, until he has mercy upon us. Have mercy upon us, O Lord, have mercy upon us, for we have had more than enough of contempt.

❖   ❖   ❖

A noted marriage researcher wrote that one of the signs he observed in relationships that were in trouble were ones which were marked with contempt. Sometimes contempt makes itself known when expressions of anger focus more on the person than on what the person did or said. Contempt might be seen when we resort to name-calling. Such contempt cuts deeper than criticism. We can imagine making course corrections on what we do, but if the problem is who we are then we have nothing to do but bleed out. To look to God is to believe in mercy and trust that with his own wounded hand, he can - and will - make our bleeding stop.

❖   ❖   ❖

Holy God, have mercy on us. Amen.

DECEMBER ◆ 12

I Thessalonians 5:9-11
For God has destined us not for wrath but for obtaining salvation through our Lord Jesus Christ, who died for us, so that whether we are awake or asleep we may live with him. Therefore encourage one another and build up each other, as indeed you are doing.

❖ ❖ ❖

The little chapel services for our early learning center include an offering. The children come forward to the altar steps and place in a large basket a picture they have colored. What amazes me is that they do it so willingly. I show my glee and joy with my clapping hands and my smiling eyes. I praise them for their acts of generosity and their joyful spirit. Praise, thanks, and joy are tougher to sell to adults who have been pounded down with ill will and harsh criticism for more days than they have ever been lifted up. Our task as disciples of a loving God is often to jump on the scale and tip the balance in the best direction.

❖ ❖ ❖

Help us, Lord, to pray for one another and encourage one another in the things that make for peace. Amen.

December ◆ 13

Matthew 25:21
His master said to him, 'Well done, good and trustworthy slave; you have been trustworthy in a few things, I will put you in charge of many things; enter into the joy of your master.'

❖ ❖ ❖

Let's call this the "Puppy Principle." Young couples will sometimes get a puppy to ease themselves into the idea of parenthood. Parents will get a puppy for their children to teach them responsibility. It makes sense to start with small responsibilities before entrusting one another with larger responsibilities. I feel sorry for the puppy who hasn't got a clue that it is a litmus test for human maturity. The puppy deserves better. As God's people, we are given responsibilities small and great. How we attend to the little things is just as important as anything else. The little thing might be a puppy of a gesture in which we do God's work.

❖ ❖ ❖

Holy God, may we attend with care those little things which you have entrusted to us. Amen.

DECEMBER ◆ 14

I Kings 17: 8-9
The word of the Lord came to Elijah, saying, "Go to Zarepheth, which belongs to Sidon, and live there for I have commanded a widow there to feed you."

❖ ❖ ❖

As it turns out, the widow woman to whom the Lord was sending Elijah was about to prepare her last meal for her and her son before becoming famine victims themselves. A house guest was not a part of their last meal plan. The Lord's command to this widow was not the stuff of voices in the night but seeded in her deep sense of hospitality to the stranger. She told Elijah she had little to give. Elijah told her to prepare food for them all. The Lord honored her act of kindness by providing her with what she needed to be hospitable. Meager meals can be major feasts when prepared with open hands and willing hearts.

❖ ❖ ❖

Lord, keep us steadfast in your word and fill us to overflowing with a river of justice. Amen.

DECEMBER ◆ 15

Deuteronomy 8:3
He humbled you by letting you hunger, then by feeding you with manna, with which neither you nor your ancestors were acquainted, in order to make you understand that one does not live by bread alone, but by every word that comes from the mouth of the Lord.

❖　　❖　　❖

A little deprivation is not a bad thing. After the hurricane, my power was off for a couple weeks. I had properly prepared provisions that did not require refrigeration or heat. I had flashlights with which I could move around the house. I had a radio to listen to the news. It was like camping inside your own house. After a while, it got old. When the first flicker of power returned, when I could prepare my first hot meal, when I could walk around the house without a flashlight, I was thrilled. I wondered how long it would take before I took for granted a light switch and a cup of hot coffee. Perhaps those times when we don't think God is anywhere in particular are purposeful events to help us remember that we would be no place in particular without him.

❖　　❖　　❖

Holy God, you are present either teaching us not to take you for granted or comforting us with your amazing grace. Amen.

DECEMBER ◆ 16

I Corinthians 9:11-12
You will be enriched in every way for your great generosity, which will produce thanksgiving to God through us; for the rendering of this ministry not only supplies the needs of the saints but also overflows with many thanksgivings to God.

❖ ❖ ❖

Someone asked for my help recently to identify a family in need or another good cause. Their large extended family had decided this year to pool their gift money and give it away rather than buy items for gifts. The juggernaut of holiday gift-shopping is upon us again. The retailers need us to shop to keep their stores open and keep people employed. Families are more likely these days to ask, "What do we really need?" rather than "What do we want?" Businesses who want to stay in business will work hard to move us from "that would be nice to have" to "that is what we have to have." We are torn with the voices of children telling us what they want. With all those voices, we need to hear a voice to guide us. God's word to us is not "Stop Giving" but give as thanksgiving to God, give with the needs of everyone in mind.

❖ ❖ ❖

Holy God, we give you thanks and praise and ask for your wisdom to discern the needs of others and to give with joy. Amen.

DECEMBER ◆ 17

Jeremiah 23:5
The days are surely coming, says the Lord, when I will raise up for David a righteous Branch, and he shall reign as king and deal wisely, and shall execute justice and righteousness in the land.

❖   ❖   ❖

There is a law office commercial that asks the question, "Do you have a deferred cash settlement but need your cash now?" and people are seen responding, "Yeah, it's my money and I need it NOW!" We are an Easter people even as we prepare for Christmas. Jesus, the branch of David, has come and died and risen again. He promised to return and reign in righteousness. I feel compelled to fling open the window, lean out and shout as loud as my voice is able, "Yeah, Lord, you are my savior and I need you NOW!" When we are plowed under a pile of daily manure, we cling to whatever clean and good thing we can find. God's promise of a new day and a new age continues, even when it is not happening on our schedule, is a golden shovel for a messy day.

❖   ❖   ❖

We wrap our hearts and hands on the handle of your promise, Lord. Amen.

DECEMBER ◆ 18

Isaiah 64:4
From ages past no one has heard, no ear has perceived, no eye has seen any God besides you, who works for those who wait for him.

❖ ❖ ❖

I have a colleague who once spoke tongue-in-cheek about how the only emotions that men really understand are good and bad. He would often write and speak with some eloquence about how much more complex women are than men especially in their range of emotions. He opined that this was why men look perplexed most of the time. I wonder if over the years of growing in our understanding the character of God, that we haven't flattened God's emotional landscape into simply good and bad. If I can imagine a God who is far more complex and that I believe that God is greater than my imagination, then I also believe that God is beyond the limitations of gender. In this Advent season we again live in a time of intentional waiting for the return of Christ. We may be wise to consider that the one for whom we wait is waiting for us.

❖ ❖ ❖

Holy God, be wildly present with us in this day so that we may grow in the knowledge of who you truly are. Amen.

DECEMBER ◆ 19

Even so, Lord quickly come
To your final harvest home.
Gather all your people in,
Free from sorrow, free from sin,
There, forever purified,
In your garner to abide.
Come, with all your angels, come,
Raise the glorious harvest home.

❖   ❖   ❖

It isn't a bit of scripture today as is my typical practice to which I will most certainly return, however, it is the last verse of "Come, You thankful people, Come" - a classic hymn that is traditionally sung at Thanksgiving. This verse is stuck in my head. When the world seems more fragile and fractured, when the economy issues have metastasized into our daily lives, when the future looks like a jungle rather than a highway, my prayers for Jesus to "quickly come" happen in earnest. The forces at work in the world have the effect of driving us away from each other and from God. We are even separated from our best selves. The Spirit of the Living God resists these forces and draw us closer to one another. May your gatherings in this season be ones in which you see and touch and taste the power of God to bless our lives with his purposes.

❖   ❖   ❖

Gather all your people in, Lord, gather all your people in. Amen.

DECEMBER ◆ 20

Isaiah 11:1-2
A shoot shall come out from the stump of Jesse, and a branch shall grow out of his roots. The spirit of the Lord shall rest on him, the spirit of wisdom and understanding, the spirit of counsel and might, the spirit of knowledge and the fear of the Lord.

❖   ❖   ❖

I was told by a visiting neighbor that I may want to consider moving a particular plant that was too close to the house. The plant's root system spreads so much and is so strong that it tends to tear up foundations. I decided to take the advice and was stunned to see how a relatively small plant had sent thick roots widely across my yard and under the patio. I had to apply some serious measures to uproot the whole plant. It wasn't the kind of plant a person would want growing too closely to one's house. But it is the kind of plant that I know the Church has been like over the years. Through the years, the Church's branches have been cut and beaten but its roots are pervasive and strong. The words of Isaiah are used in our baptismal liturgy which is at the root of our faith. When in doubt, we are wise to go back to our roots.

❖   ❖   ❖

Holy God, we give thanks for the strong roots you have given us for the foundation of our faith. Amen.

DECEMBER ◆ 21

Psalm 72:1-4
Give the king your justice, O God, and your righteousness to a king's son. May he judge your people with righteousness, and your poor with justice. May the mountains yield prosperity for the people, and the hills, in righteousness. May he defend the cause of the poor of the people, give deliverance to the needy, and crush the oppressor.

❖ ❖ ❖

We know what we want from our leaders. We want justice. We want someone who can make a decision that will be right. We know that we want a leader who defends those in need because at any given time, that may be us. We want justice, but are often unwilling or ill-equipped to know how to make it happen. There are those who hide in the shadows hoping that someone else will take the lead. There are those who dive into the fray and take on a cause. The cause may be overwhelming, just the tip of the iceberg, but there are those willing to chip away at it nonetheless because it is the right thing to do. God has given us himself in Jesus as the champion for justice that we need. We can hide from, lead, or follow those we know who walk in righteousness.

❖ ❖ ❖

Almighty God, chase us from the shadows of fear into the light of justice. Amen.

DECEMBER ◆ 22

Romans 15:4-6
For whatever was written in former days was written for our instruction, so that by steadfastness and by the encouragement of the scriptures we might have hope. May the God of steadfastness and encouragement grant you to live in harmony with one another, in accordance with Christ Jesus, so that together you may with one voice glorify the God and Father of our Lord Jesus Christ.

❖   ❖   ❖

Harmony for harmony's sake is often a good motivation to get along with difficult people. Use it as a motivator too often and we get tired of it. Put any group of people together and they will experience conflict. If they fight all the time then their identity in the world is marked by that conflict. As followers together of Jesus, there is a larger purpose for working for peace with one another. It is in being able to present an authentic, united witness to the world of God's purposes. A divided house cannot stand and a divided community of faith is a poor witness. Peace is not absence of sin and brokenness but the presence of love, the steadfast belief in the power of forgiveness. Ignoring the wounds and putting on a mask of wholeness is a lie that the world can easily recognize. The wholeness we seek is in Christ Jesus and it is that wholeness that witnesses best to a broken world.

❖   ❖   ❖

Dear Lord, help us to confront our brokenness, apply the healing power of your grace and witness to a world in need. Amen.

DECEMBER ◆ 23

Isaiah 35:10
And the ransomed of the Lord shall return, and come to Zion with singing; everlasting joy shall be upon their heads; they shall obtain joy and gladness, and sorrow and sighing shall flee away.

❖ ❖ ❖

It is hard to know how to live well in the land between Christmas lights and the reality of death that comes through acts of human violence or insidious little cancer cells. Between absolute delight and utter despair is where most of us live from day to day, learning to keep the pendulum from swinging too closely to the edges where we cannot or dare not linger. We are the ones saved by the living God to bear witness to his grace. We do that sometimes by singing and sometimes by simply by living one day to the next. Jesus is here. Jesus is coming again.

❖ ❖ ❖

Come, Lord, and let your joyous light shine. Amen.

DECEMBER ◆ 24

Psalm 146:1-4
Praise the Lord! Praise the Lord, O my soul! I will praise the Lord as long as I live; I will sing praises to my God all my life long. Do not put your trust in princes, in mortals, in whom there is no help. When their breath departs, they return to the earth; on that very day their plans perish.

❖ ❖ ❖

Popular phrase says, "If you want to make God laugh, tell him your plans." We blaze ahead with our own agenda and we may even give God a passing glance. We may show God our plans and ask him to shake a little blessing on it like blowing on a set of dice for luck. Then we plow on with our own agenda. One of the catch phrases of our culture is "Control freak." We recognize one when we see one. None of us wants to be one. But needing control is the nature of our sinful selves. I feel better about the days when I pray that I will not get in God's way than when I try to wrestle for control.

❖ ❖ ❖

Holy God, may I be inside your will today. Amen.

DECEMBER ◆ 25

James 5:8-10
You also must be patient. Strengthen your hearts, for the coming of the Lord is near. Beloved, do not grumble against one another, so that you may not be judged. See, the Judge is standing at the doors! As an example of suffering and patience, beloved, take the prophets who spoke in the name of the Lord.

❖   ❖   ❖

This passage sounds more like parent talking to a child about Santa Claus. Patience, he's coming! Naughty and nice! Parents have to work at teaching and motivating their children for good behavior, especially the kind of behavior that resists the temptation to think only of ourselves. Sadly, we are still working on that behavior as adults, but we don't have the parent over our shoulder correcting us and encouraging us along the way. We have to do that for one another. And so we lift one another up in thoughts and prayers so that we can become the best of who we are intended to be. We receive the gift of the Christ child at Christmas so that we can be a gift to the world.

❖   ❖   ❖

Holy God, for the witness of disciples, friends and family, we give you thanks for their encouragement. Amen.

DECEMBER ◆ 26

Matthew 11:2-6
When John heard in prison what the Messiah was doing, he sent word by his disciples and said to him, "Are you the one who is to come, or are we to wait for another?" Jesus answered them, "Go and tell John what you hear and see: the blind receive their sight, the lame walk, the lepers are cleansed, the deaf hear, the dead are raised, and the poor have good news brought to them. And blessed is anyone who takes no offense at me."

❖   ❖   ❖

One of the great perks of my job is that I get to talk and to hear about God all the time. People expect me to do the "God talk" and help people make connections with the God who seeks out a relationship with them. People feel free to share with me where they have witnessed the power of God in their lives because they know I will not dismiss them or think them crazy. John the Baptist sitting in prison was isolated from the witness of God's spirit alive in the world. He needed to hear what God was doing. We are simply asked to tell what we have seen and heard. I have seen lives changed, I have seen hope even in the midst of brokenness and mourning. I have seen weary marriages sparkle like a new diamond. I have seen the power of a new day despite the darkness of the night. Go and tell what you have seen and heard.

❖   ❖   ❖

Holy God, shine on us and give us the words to tell what we have known to be true. Amen.

DECEMBER ◆ 27

Isaiah 7:14
Therefore the Lord himself will give you a sign. Look, the young woman is with child and shall bear a son, and shall name him Immanuel.

❖ ❖ ❖

Those of us who have never had children can wax poetic about the simplicity of a child as a sign to the nations of God's power and reign on earth. Those who have children know that a child can immediately introduce complications to a household in seismic proportions. Just taking a child out into the world on an errand requires the strength and stamina of a Sherpa. God took his infant son out into the world for the errand of saving it. The sign of a parent with a child is a miracle no matter how we look at it. God comes in power and strength.

❖ ❖ ❖

Holy God, we rest in your powerful arms and we rediscover the miracle of your love. Amen.

DECEMBER ◆ 28

Psalm 80:8-12
You brought a vine out of Egypt; you drove out the nations and planted it. You cleared the ground for it; it took deep root and filled the land. The mountains were covered with its shade, the mighty cedars with its branches; it sent out its branches to the sea, and its shoots to the River. Why then have you broken down its walls, so that all who pass along the way pluck its fruit?

❖   ❖   ❖

I appreciate the boldness of the psalmist to speak to God with such a major attitude. "YOU did this and YOU did that and now YOU are allowing all this bad stuff to happen." We are so often quick to blame and slow to take responsibility for our own circumstances. If God is the source of all blessing then it seems fair that everything else is his doing as well. That would make us empty spectators or puppets in a drama that would have no other point than to amuse the puppet master. Instead of puppets, we are embraced as children who need guidance and wisdom, patience and love to see ourselves and our world differently. Of the many things God does, the most profound act is that of a loving parent listening to his pouting children.

❖   ❖   ❖

You, O Lord, are the one to whom we run when we are weary, lonely, confused and frustrated. Thank you for your ceaseless love. Amen.

December ◆ 29

Isaiah 9:2
The people who walked in darkness have seen a great light; those who lived in a land of deep darkness- on them light has shined.

❖   ❖   ❖

Flying over a city at night, I have always been struck by how feeble our attempts of lighting the darkness. From the air, our street lamps seem like flashlights with low batteries. Our lights are so small and the night so vast. During the Christmas season we did our best to lighten the darkness, but it is not always that easy to rise to the joy of the season. We cannot always do it for very long. Our batteries of our spirit do get low. However, it does not take much light to shine on a human face. We are given all that we truly need in a babe in a manger and a guiding star. The darkness shall not overcome the light that God has brought into the world.

❖   ❖   ❖

Holy God, may we reflect the light of your gracious love. Amen.

December ◆ 30

Isaiah 40:7-8
The grass withers, the flower fades, when the breath of the Lord blows upon it; surely the people are grass. The grass withers, the flower fades; but the word of our God will stand forever.

❖   ❖   ❖

I am not, nor will ever be, a lawn ranger. I have a lawn and I naively expect that if the lawn is mowed and watered it will do what lawns are supposed to do. I expect that a lawn will make the house look nice and shame the neighbors into mowing their lawns. I have learned that grass is more fragile and requires higher maintenance than I imagined. It needs a fairy sod mother to ward off weeds and insects and monitor the weather. It is little wonder to me why the prophet compares us to grass. We are just as fragile and needy. We can sink our roots only so far into the soil to find water. We have no weapons against some enemies but whether we live or whether we die, we are the Lord's.

❖   ❖   ❖

Feed and nourish us, O Lord, that we might be a witness to your steadfast love. Amen.

DECEMBER ◆ 31

John 3:15-16
For God so loved the world that he gave his only Son, so that everyone who believes in him may not perish but may have eternal life. Indeed, God did not send the Son into the world to condemn the world, but in order that the world might be saved through him.

❖ ❖ ❖

Martin Luther, the man who wrote volumes of commentaries on the scriptures, called this verse of scripture "the Gospel in a nutshell." Luther could never imagine an age in which our attention span has been so shortened that we would, in fact, need a shortened version of the Gospel message. One long-time subscriber to ELOGOS once confessed to me that though they longed to read their Bible every day, they just could not find the time or the discipline to stick with it. My response was, "But you read ELOGOS every day and that includes scripture!" The person was surprised and relieved to discover a discipline he didn't know he already possessed. He just thought that reading the Bible everyday meant reading alot of it in one sitting. Even if the knowledge of Jesus comes to us in small ways, it can still strengthen us for the journey. These verses from John's Gospel bear witness to the power of God at work in a few, short words. I pray that this book of devotions has been a delivery system for God's powerful word in your life. May your new year be filled with opportunities for you to be a blessing to others.

❖ ❖ ❖

Precious Lord, may we live your word of love for all around us today. Amen.

About the Author

Deb Grant was born in Massachusetts and lived with her family in Agawam, Massachusetts until leaving for college in Rhode Island. She graduated from Barrington College in 1975 with an under-graduate degree in English and Biblical Studies. Grant started seminary at Gordon-Conwell Theological Seminary in Massachusetts and transferred to Trinity Lutheran Seminary in Columbus, Ohio where she earned her Masters of Divinity degree in 1981.

Grant was ordained as a pastor in the American Lutheran Church (now ELCA) on September 6, 1981. Since then, she has served congregations in Tennessee, South Carolina and Texas. Her ministry career includes being the Lutheran campus pastor at Clemson University and Texas A&M University.

Grant's other publications include *Pedestrian Theology, The Jesse Tree* (Creative Communications for the Parish), ELOGOS Daily Devotions for Down to Earth Disciples 1 & 2. She has also written for the devotional periodical *Christ in our Home* and frequently contributes to *Word in Season* (Augsburg Fortress).

Deb Grant continues to write ELOGOS as a daily email devotional to which anyone may subscribe. To subscribe to ELOGOS emails go to:
www.elogosdailydevotions.com.
Deb Grant can be contacted by email:
revdeb@jazzwater.com

Other Works by Deb Grant

Pedestrian Theology
Langmarc Publishing, 2005
Amazon.com

What readers are saying:
"Deb Grant offers her story—at once filled with humor and pathos, sin and sanctification—as a gift to all of us "pedestrians" who are trying to make sense of our own walks through life. The book tells the truth in a style that echoes Frederick Buechner and Walter Wangerin, Jr. It is a book for everyone who has suffered loss, faced their demons, and reached for God and for all who want to assist others in doing the same."
—*Dr. Brad A. Binau, Trinity Lutheran Seminary, Columbus, Ohio*

"Whether you are a doubter searching for assurance or a believer craving insight, Pedestrian Theology delivers a unique road map to a faithful life. Through wit, artistry, and raw introspection, Deb Grant reveals what it means to be found by God, saved by the cross, and liberated by love. This exploration of original sin, forgiveness, and faith is a picture of a life grounded in grace."
—*Dr. Erika Abel, Baylor University, Waco, Texas*

ELOGOS
Daily Devotions for Down to Earth Disciples
Winner – USA Best Books Awards
Prayer and Devotionals
Finalist – NIEA Book Awards
Spirituality